# GOD AND SEX

PREVIOUS BOOKS BY MARK WHITWELL

*Yoga of Heart* (Lantern Books, 2004)
*The Promise* (Atria Books, 2012)
*The Hridayayogasutra* (Urban Family, 2012)

Praise for *Yoga of Heart*

"Here comes the Sun. It's all right. We are not separate from what it's all about. Please listen to Mark. Breathe. Feel it. He'll show you. He knows a way. By the Grace of the Sun."
— Richie Havens

"A global view and the technical detail for everybody. A simple message profoundly delivered. Read this book."
— Baron Baptiste, author of *Journey into Power*

"Contemporary, hip, and ancient, Mark is stepping lightly in the footsteps of the Masters. A remarkable Yoga text and the perfect companion to Desikachar's The Heart of Yoga."
— Shiva Rea, author of *Tending the Heart Fire*

Finally, yoga as it should be taught. With purity and straight from the heart. Mark gently reminds us that we ARE here now."
— Christy Turlington Burns

Praise for *The Promise*

"Indeed a soft message for a hard time . . . God is in this moment. God is as close as your own breath. So be here now! Mark will show you an easy way."

— Ram Dass, author of *Be Here Now*

"In his book, Mark shares the importance of breathing to energize ourselves. Breathe and let go. Read this book."

— Deepak Chopra

"Mark Whitwell offers readers a sensitive and very inspiring approach to a topic that matters to everyone. This is a lovely book."

— Caroline Myss, author of *Anatomy of the Spirit*

"Inhale the wisdom of this book, and exhale its practices into the sacredness of your everyday activities."

— Michael Bernard Beckwith, author of *Spiritual Liberation* and founder of *Agape*

"Now in seven simple minutes you can transform your breath, your mind, your love, your intimacy and certainly your sex life."

— Dr. John Demartini, author of *The Heart of Love*

"Whitwell's teachings are a path not just to greater intimacy in relationships, but also to a greater intimacy with all of life."

— Larry Dossey, MD, author of *Reinventing Medicine*

"Kudos to Mark for this intimate step to love and sex! Intimacy and sex should indeed be synonymous."

— C. Norman Shealy, MD, PhD, author of *Energy Medicine*

"I have prescribed Mark's breathing and movement routine to hundreds of my patients, who have reported a renaissance of energy in their lives, while experiencing deeper sleep, a stronger body composition, more vitality, less depression, and an astonishingly improved sensuality and sex drive."

— Prudence Hall, MD, founder of the Hall Center

# GOD AND SEX

## *now we get both*

Mark Whitwell

*with*

Andy Raba & Rosalind Atkinson

Silver Snake Press

God and Sex: Now We Get Both



In collaboration with Andy Raba and Rosalind Atkinson



First published May 2019
Revised July 2019
Hardcover edition published December 2019

ISBN: 978-0-473-48591-7

Cataloguing Data: Whitwell, Mark, author.
God and Sex: Now We Get Both (2019). Spirituality -- Relationships -- Social Criticism -- Philosophy. ISBN: 978-0-473-48591-7 (hardcover).

Published by Silver Snake Press, Wellington, New Zealand

www.silversnakepress.com

www.godandsex.com

Silver Snake Press

*I dedicate this book to you, the reader.*
*You are the power of the cosmos, arising as pure intelligence and unspeakable beauty. You are in perfect and intrinsic harmony and dependence with every aspect of the cosmos. This is a fact, not a spiritual statement or a poem. This book is for you, so that you may enjoy this fact, the reality of your own existence in your natural state.*

# CONTENTS

# ACKNOWLEDGEMENTS

Andy Raba and Rosalind Atkinson's love of life and dedication to freeing humanity to feel our intrinsic peace and power has moved them to make their vital contributions to this book. Their real life experiences—honest stories of difficulty, transformation, and victory—and those of many friends and family members around the globe gave the substance and reality to these pages. To all of them I am very grateful.

We give you, the reader, our collective experience of what our teachers gave to us. We thank you for receiving these gifts with us. May we get the job done together.

To my first teachers, my beloved parents, to all the great ones who appeared in my life, and to the entire wisdom tradition of humanity across all cultures, all times and all geographies... I bow down.

# FIRST WORDS

I READ RECENTLY THAT THE PEOPLE WHO ARE MOST HELPFUL TO US IN our lives are those who can perceive underlying patterns in the chaos of daily existence. These are our prophets, who care to look deeper into the mess and deftly intervene with the innocence and lightness of a child asking "But why?" Why does the God concept, which is supposedly all about love, inspire so much violence? Why do people flinch when you say "Sex"? Why are our relationships so fraught and complicated compared to those of any other animal? Why do we seem hell-bent on destroying the systems that support us, whether in our own bodies or in the body of the earth? Why do I feel so bad?

The prophet is not someone who knows what is going to happen; she or he is someone who has explored the logics of human life and observed that when we do X, it leads to Y. This can be all of us. We are all moved to lessen human suffering for ourselves and others, and this book gives us a framework to perceive the mess as one unfolding and preventable disaster, rather than a series of inevitable events. This writing is agency that will allow us to intervene effectively. As it says in the Christian canon, "Would God that all the Lord's people were prophets."

In this book, Mark dares to address the root pattern from which the dysfunction of our religious and relational lives springs: the separation of God and Sex. It is a separation both powerful and imaginary; it has wreaked havoc through human life and yet does not exist at all. God and Sex are more than two abstract concepts, or two interests that a person with a little spare time may hold. They point to the entire human conception of what is sacred and what is not. There is a reason why the great English mystic, William Blake, chose to end poems with the triumphant exclamation, "Everything that lives is Holy!" It is because what we perceive to be sacred is what we will treat with reverence and care. To put it another way, the grotesque impulse to dominate the world relies on perceiving it in certain deadened ways. How we see and how we act are inseparably intertwined.

And yet, this is not a work of social criticism. It is activism, yes, but it is primarily an invitation to love life, yours and mine. Mark might say, "to feel *better* and to *feel* better, two different sentences." To cognize that God is already arising as your hands holding this book and your eyes perceiving the shapes of the letters and translating them into concepts in your beautiful mind. And to realize that life is Sex. It is the fundamental creative energy of embodied existence, not a problematic, exaggerated, scarce, or dangerous hobby to be giggled and grieved over with ghoulish fascination. This book invites you into an entirely Sex-positive life that is serious about pleasure as a refined and radical force in this world. If you are looking for some kind of vulgar handbook, I'm afraid you will be disappointed. Sex is the heart's activity, and so our primary business is to discard whatever obstructs the heart, enabling life to flow spontaneously in the directions she pleases.

Mark's project is not to add to your conceptualizations, but rather to plant logics that will cause existing ideas that do not serve us to self-destruct. They can depart from our minds either quickly or gradually, leaving us free to enjoy our lives. I sincerely hope that these words will enter your mind as both a healing balm and a gentle challenge. The virus of separative thinking inherited from dysfunctional culture has gone deep into us, and there will perhaps be a little heat as it leaves. To anyone who has been called to question their life more deeply: this book is for you, and for all humanity. May you find this book both useful and provocative in your explorations of life.

There is real friendship in these words. I love Mark, and I love our collaborator Andy Raba, because they are not trying to be 'right,' but sincerely wishing to help people. My profound gratitude to Mark for clarifying these matters for myself and everyone.

*Rosalind Atkinson*
Palm Springs, California, May 2019

# INTRODUCTION

GOD AND SEX: THE TWO MOST POWERFUL AND MISUNDERSTOOD words in the English language. In the presumed separation between these words, each has denied and toxified the other. Now, placed together, each will purify and empower the other. In this book we bring them together, clarifying the meaning of both words through their deep, yet profoundly simple convergence.

For most of the public, each of these words has uneasy connotations and evokes a complicated response. The pervasive idea of God as 'other' creates either fanatical adherence to or fanatical rejection of the God-concept—or just a casual turning-away, because it is too hard or irrelevant to think about. Likewise, the word Sex usually implies a compromise: something negative, something sleazy, something desperate and inaccessible, or something that is fundamentally disappointing. Notice how in the English language, God is usually capitalized, but 'sex' not, showing the implicit hierarchy.* For both loaded words, there is exaggerated response, or denial, or oscillation between the two.

Yet God is Sex. Creation is Sex. We, and all of life, were all literally created through Sex. Our life is about participation in that beauty, that source, and therefore requires right relationship and right sexuality. But the social behaviors around Sex don't match up with this. Look at the beauty that is you. The way nature is blooming as your whole body. Look at the power that is you. Your parents probably did not consciously participate in this, but nevertheless they are that. Sex, the

---

* We attempt to address this implied hierarchy through the capitalization of 'Sex' throughout this book, rather than the potentially offensive decapitalization of 'God.'

complete union of male-female polarity,* is the way life renews itself, regenerates and evolves all species. Is that not God's method on Earth? Is not the means of 'the creator'—indeed, the basis of all creation—the union and attraction of opposites? Think about how all plants, animals, insects, fungi, and other life forms duplicate themselves. No one enters this realm without Sex. It is entirely God's purpose and can be enjoyed and participated in as the profundity of that purpose. It is a big and profound word, the heart's activity, not the exaggerated physical activity popularized by the burden of pornography or merely the socio-religious duty of procreation. In this book, you will have an alternative framework to cognize the meaning of Sex (and God) in your life.

***

I was born into a society that had very fixed ideas about God and very perverse ideas and behaviors around Sex. In my life of exploration in the cultures around the planet, I saw that it was universally true that the idea of God as 'other' was making everybody miserable. Man's idea of heaven had created a hell of this abundant paradise. Yet in my explorations of the great cultural wisdoms of humanity, I've found that the word 'God' can and has been used to refer to the unspeakable beauty and depthless wonder that is every day of life on Earth. Not to God as 'other,' as a distant controlling source or abstract father figure requiring paranoia and obedience. But 'God' as a word to refer to the supreme beauty, intelligence, power, and wonder of our 'ordinary' life and the vast intrinsic harmony of how this cosmos functions. Terrible

---

* Throughout this book, I talk about Sex / God / Life as the intrinsic male-female collaboration: male-female in the sense of ancient personifications for the two forces in union that make up our reality, not referring to male or female bodies or any kind of cultural gender patterning or behavior. Talking about the characteristics of 'the masculine' or 'the feminine' is in no way referring to characteristics of men versus women. In this book, we are not drawing essentialist divides that posit woman as of the earth and man as of spirit or anything like that. Such divisions are themselves reinforcing the artificial divide between God and Sex. We are all male-female, in every cell and in perfect harmony, and all Sex is participation in this primordial force, whether it be same-sex or opposite-sex intimacy, wherever we fall on or off the spectrums of body and gender identification. If this language doesn't work for you, feel free to mentally substitute with yin-yang or another cultural framework of opposites in union.

things have been justified using this simple three-letter word; rather than abandon it altogether, we can purify it by bringing it back down to earth to refer to the power that is alive as you and me and everything that exists.

On the other hand, I saw that Sex and the common behaviors associated with the word had been reduced to vulgarity and at worse abuse. Wherever I went, it was not forming the basis of an intelligent sensitive human life, even though it was obvious to me that Sex was the basis of all life, the means by which we all got here, and Mother Nature's primary interest in her mission to generate and evolve all species. It was absurd to see how human life around the world had been formed from the denial of Sex. In my explorations, however, I found faint traces of examples in the ancient history of humanity in which sexual practice was participation in the fact of our perfect wonder—an understanding and practice unknown to most of modern society. I intend for this book to inform our vast public of how to restore real God to our lives, and real and honest Sex as our participation in and enactment of God on Earth.

True spiritual practice (which just means true enjoyment and free participation in life) is embodied: it is participation in the union of opposites within and without, where one empowers the other in endless mutual exchange. Spiritual life (i.e., fully human life) is not about transcending this world, but about participation in this perfect union of the feminine and the masculine principles. It therefore requires right relationship and rightful sexuality simply because they are a part of life—or rather, because they *are* life. Sexuality is treated as an antithetical, embarrassing, or too-painful side event to the main business of spirituality and 'God.' Or else it is exaggerated in the belief that it is unimportant or will help us towards some imagined sublimity—or to feel something, at least. But profound consideration of these matters is the heart of God-realization, the absolutely essential concern for us to investigate and resolve. Why? Because Sex is the substance of reality itself, the attraction of equal opposites that creates life and synchronistically abides as the nurturing and regenerative force of life. So it must be honored and made completely positive, real, and honest.

The dreadful weight of religious and spiritual teachings has been an attempt to overcome the natural force of sexuality as if it is an obstacle to realization of 'higher' matters. We have all encountered the painful results of the culturally engrained assumption that Sex is 'lower.' This assumption is a great burden on humanity. From here, the patriarchal method has been to propose effort towards 'higher' future realities. The resulting hierarchical systems are the denial of life itself as it is given. Our human lives can and must be restored as pure participation in the already-present nurturing flow of life, free of any power structures or hierarchical impositions.

It may appear that modern rationality and science have largely replaced the ancient religious thought structures, and that it is no longer relevant to talk about the impact of God ideas. Yet the basic (imaginary) split between 'God' as controlling force over and above the tangible realities of Sex/Body/Earth has never been healed. It remains in the thought structures of culture, with mind now generally taking the role of the transcendent superior force. Our bodies and Sex are still assumed to be less. The feminine is still assumed to be less. The Earth is still assumed to be an unintelligent resource. We are seeing the destructive results of this set of beliefs like never before. When we assume creativity and purposeful intelligence are outside of the physical, we are left with a mechanical, knowable world that we attempt to master and control, creating the environmental crisis amongst many other personal and political dysfunctions. The scientific paradigm turns the world (and our own bodies) into a bland place and produces a feeling and identity of apparent separation as mere observers or exploiters. We think we are people who observe nature rather than nature itself. It is the same old religious split between God and Sex in a modified form. It does not represent recognition of the obvious wholeness and holiness of our own present situation; it leaves us still believing there is something lacking in normal existence and searching for future possibilities.

The search for future happiness, perfection, or a painless existence are all modern forms of the engrained search to escape Sex and get to God. Even modern forms of sexual exaggeration are paradoxically a denial of Sex, as they attempt to use novelty and stimulation to compensate for a lack of depth of intimacy and feeling. Whether it is framed in the religious language of 'God-realization' or 'enlightenment' or in the secular mode of self-improvement and progress, the habitual denial of our given reality ruins lives. Everywhere we look, we see friends and family in a state of confusion and estrangement, moving through their lives filled with quiet despair and addiction. We want to help them, but without addressing the root of the problem, which is the sense of disconnection from our actual reality, we are left feeling powerless. The solution given by traditional and new-age religious and spiritual teachers alike is to present themselves as another ideal to be replicated. Yet the model of the perfect person implies once again that everyone else is not perfect, and so only adds to our suffering. It stimulates the struggle in arbitrary criteria towards self-improvement by which we measure ourselves as winners or losers.

I have observed that when people are not given the experience of their inherent connection to life in every aspect including the fact that everything is arising from Sex, they can go insane. Humanity is presently experiencing this terror in the form of everything from mild despair and depression through to outbursts of atrocity from the clinically insane. Our social inheritance is a needless war of mind over body, which is stored in every cell of the body and can be the direct cause of degenerative illness, anxiety, and depression. Society then blames the individual for their unhappiness or illness, all the while refusing to reckon with the fundamentally life-denying thought structures that underpin modern culture. Mental illness symptoms are usually met with mind-over-matter ideologies that encourage us to simply repeat positive slogans over and over again in our heads: "Today is a good day to have a good day!" "I am love," "I choose to enjoy this moment," *et cetera*. While thoughts do have an impact on our emotions and mood, these banal catchphrases do nothing to address or critically reflect upon the underlying assumptions of both religious belief systems and their direct offspring, secular consumer society—the religion of money, productivity, and self-improvement. We feel like our suffering is a personal failure, when really so much of it stems from cultural errors that were imposed on us. I hope this book can show how we are all in this together—we were all brainwashed, and yet we are all still nevertheless the embodiment of both God and Sex, and can step free from the burden of the idea that they are separate at any moment. To be clear, it is the idea that we are separate from ourselves, from nature and from the power of the cosmos that causes so much suffering and seems to rob us of our lives. Positive thinking psychology can effect a doubling down of this logic by demanding that the mind should just reassert itself over the legitimate suffering of the whole body, further overriding the body's feeling-intelligence. When we stop listening to the body in this way, we inevitably crash against the rocks. This book is for anyone who wants to discover real and honest positivity in their life through dissolving our inherited negative thought structures, rather than candy-coating them in hopefulness.

I am feeling a deep sympathy for everyOne who is doing their best to make society function and feeling alone amidst relationship dysfunction. I feel great sympathy for everyOne suffering these chronic limitations, and I hope this book can illustrate to you how they are not your fault, but rather the cultural patterns into which we were born. There is a way through, and it is your direct embrace/participation in the given reality, the beauty, the intelligence, and the harmony that is existence itself. It is your birthright. No-one need give this to you, and no-one can take it away. Freedom from aimless wandering comes with the understanding that reality is our being. We are liberated into our own lives, waking down *into* real life not waking up out of it. When we bring God and Sex together and see that their meaning is always already defined in relationship, we allow the natural state of affairs to become the basis of our life.

This book is not an alternative religious point of view. I respect the sincerity of all people in the idealisms of their comforting religious and secular identities. I do not propose any new religious or secular identity, but rather offer the understanding to actualize human ideals and make them useful, instead of being part of a torturous search. I encourage you to read this book and bring God to your understanding of Sex, and Sex to your understanding of God. Both will be purified. This book is a reminder, over and over again, that you are the perfect power of Life, already. You are not less than that. It needs to be said over and over again until every body is deprogrammed from the crippling assumption of lack. Consider this book a deprogramming device. You will stand in your own ground.

If the ideas in this book are a challenge to your sincerely held views and feelings, I stand with you as a friend with respect for your feelings and ask that we go through this together. The cultural division of God and Sex has gone into us like an intractable virus, and like any healing process, there can be discomfort as the virus leaves us. It might get quite hot at times, like a fever! But my intention is not to make an argument for anything at all; but to set people free from this virus within their own traditions, allowing them to renew and embrace these traditions with renewed clarity and vigor.

*Mark Whitwell*
Aotearoa / New Zealand, April 2019

CHAPTER ONE

# *The Secrets of the Universe Are In You, As You*

*Urge and urge and urge,*
*Always the procreant urge of the world.*

*Out of the dimness opposite equals advance,*
*always substance and increase, always sex,*
*Always a knit of identity, always distinction, always a breed of life.*

*To elaborate is no avail, learn'd and unlearn'd feel that it is so.*

*Sure as the most certain sure, plumb in the uprights,*
*well entretied, braced in the beams,*
*Stout as a horse, affectionate, haughty, electrical,*
*I and this mystery here we stand.*

—Walt Whitman, *Song of Myself, 3*

IN OUR NATURAL STATE, HUMANS HAVE A WONDERFUL CIRCUMSTANCE. We have these upright soft bodies with the ability to feel deeply, especially through the frontal line. We have a very evolved nervous system and spine that culminates in a massive brain core. It is capable of many delicious functions, including self-expression, art, music, logic, feeling, Sex, and creative pleasures of all kinds. With our soft bodies and huge brain cores we can feel and enjoy our reality. We empower each other. The whole body is a feeling mechanism built entirely for relationship, especially intimate sexual union. Here there is peace, wisdom, and fullness.

But relationship is not something that we have to search for. Rather we enter into this world already and always in relationship, utterly connected to and made up of the nurturing flow of life, in union with each other and all tangible and intangible aspects of the cosmos. In the close observations of science, we see the poles of negative and positive energy functioning at atomic level, attracted and attached to one another in precise form. In our most expansive view, we see the grand orchestration of suns and planets moving in the same attraction of opposite poles holding one another in the mystery patterns of known and unknown stars. An intelligence, function, and beauty is operating in the world we know that is beyond comprehension. That same intelligence is also present in our human life in each beautiful person, in heartbeat, in breath, and in Sex. This attraction of opposites, the male-female or yin-yang equation of life, is how we all got here. It continues to move as the absolute power of life that sustains us all, and renews and nourishes us. This is the nurturing flow of the universe. And we can completely trust and participate in it. We already are it!

We are alive in this vast process, so we may as well relax. Our present body and all its relatedness is the current expression of that process. We do not have to find anything. We do not have to go crazy trying to realize it or get enlightened. Once you admit that you are the power of the cosmos, you don't need to re-realize it; you simply understand it. We don't need to carry it around or worry about forgetting it or whether we are feeling it all the time. Relationship does not have to be achieved, it just is. This is not poetry or spiritual language. It is simply the fact of our given situation, a description of the ecologies of Mother Nature. Ecology is relationship. There are no steps to be taken. We can move through life understanding that it is about participation in the given reality, not an arduous project of self-improvement. We do not have to struggle to attain a relationship with nature, life, or God, relate in a particular way, or achieve any kind of 'higher' or better state, as if we are somehow not in relatedness already!

Life is only about relationship. Only. The mind is for relationship only. It is not made to look for higher states or to constantly improve upon itself or the body. Such activity puts thought structures in the mind that obliterate its ability to notice that it is indeed arising from the heart of life as a function of life. The mind is not separate from the whole body and the whole body is not separate from Life. Imagining that mind has an existence of its own, thinking and assuming separation from its source, is like seeing a mirage. It seems to be there. But it's not really there. The mind is an unfathomable refinement of the nervous system arising from its core, the heart. It has no life or purpose dissociated from its source. It is the communication mechanism of the whole body only, designed for relationship only. It's there to say "I love you" and "Pass the biscuits." Life is to be in our own bodies, with the head/mind returned to its beautiful place as a function of the heart.

The first human right is to be intimate with our own life: the power of this universe that is arising as the whole body in pristine intrinsic harmony with the whole cosmos. It is through being intimate with the profundity of our tangible reality that our system throws out the thought structures that distract us from the given situation. When we are intimate with life as it currently stands in all the joy and pain that we hold, thought structures of a future reality are *felt* to be no longer relevant and so fall away. We only have to sweep our bodies with breath or enter honest sexual embrace to have a direct experience of our wholeness and our perfection, which is already completely established in us, as us. The unitary movement of body, breath, mind, and life ends the mirage of dissociated mind. The whole body, of course, is life. The intelligence, power, and beauty of life become the basis of mind.

When the thought structures of lack have gone deeply into us, we do often need some remedial practices of moving and breathing to reestablish ourselves in this reality. I teach this around the world and have seen many people relieved as they realize they *are* the power of the cosmos already and therefore don't have to perpetually work on themselves to become 'something' as if they are not already something. They stop insulting nature by assuming she is not doing a good enough job already in their own case.

The life current arises from the heart and now flows through the spine; it is in every cell of the body. We don't have to do anything about that. It is made abundantly available all the time. You have been graced to have received a human birth. What are the chances of that? You are unfolding in the perfect radiance of life, just like every plant is grace unfolding in the perfect radiance of life. We are not separate from nature. We are nature. And nothing is required: no meditating, no yoga, no stillness of mind, no philosophy, no places to get to, not beyond, not higher, not deeper. That is all distracting us from the fact that life is utterly given and comes perfectly delivered. You don't even need to read this book or these sentences; it is all already true of you. The truth of life is already established. There is no need for a teaching. Everything worth knowing is known already* by the intelligence of the whole body. This living organism has its own perfection, along with everything else in nature. Happiness arises when we relax into the reality of our natural condition. The secrets of the universe are already in us as us.

Please let this be the framework within which you consider everything else in this book. Stop looking, start living, start participating in the given reality as it is, in all aspects including Sex. Then you will know God.

---

* If you want to learn Chinese or how to play the guitar like Jimi Hendrix, that's okay too. But no necessity.

# CHAPTER TWO

# *So What the Hell Happened?*

*We insist that the luxuriance of nature offers itself to the person who solicits it without the desire to pillage or violate. From it comes (as if come from the depths of history and the individual) the breath of an unextinguishable desire, a harmony between beings and things, so simply present in the air at any time.*

—Raoul Vaneigem

So given this wonderful circumstance, why are the social conditions that we are born into not designed to help us enjoy our perfection? Why aren't we wandering around in this beautiful paradise, enjoying the natural pleasures of our born condition? Why does everything seem to be such a struggle? Why are so many atrocities committed in the name of God, and why has Sex become associated with abuse, pain, fear, vulgarity, scarcity, complication, shame, crass humor, or despair? Haven't we made progress to release the grip of religious fundamentalism and life-denial on society—so why are we still so unhappy? Everyone should now be allowed to freely enjoy and participate in the wonder of their own life—so what the hell has happened?

### The Orthodox Movement Away From Ordinary Conditions

Deep in the wisdom traditions of humanity is the non-dual idea that 'the Source' and 'the Seen' are One. That the Source has become Seen. Or in Christian parlance, creation and creator are One: 'On Earth as it is in heaven.' If the Source and the Seen are one, then the Seen as it is must be full and sufficient and all that is required to be with and to know the Source, to know God.

Our ancestors also recognized that the toil and survival needs of the everyday world made it difficult for people to acknowledge themselves as manifestations of this same Spirit or Source. The knowledge of interdependence could be lost. And so the ancient masters developed practices to combat the illusion that people were separate from the Earth, separate from those around them, and separate from their Source. These everyday practices were shared freely so that this truth could blossom inside of everyone. They formed the foundation from which all other religious and spiritual life arose. The intention of these practices was simple but magnificent: to establish an unending intimacy with life, nature, and God, within everyday, ordinary existence.

Unfortunately for everybody, over time religious teachings were dissociated from their origins in egalitarian, non-hierarchical society. Primordial wisdom cultures wove the poetry of 'masculine as awareness' and 'feminine as energy' together to describe the fabric of reality. Deep and charming religious philosophies then arose that warped this language into the thought structures of world religions. They took what had been a non-hierarchical framework and reimagined it to suggest that an absent God could be realized by conquering and denying what is manifest for the idea of what is prior to arising conditions. The result was a denial of arising conditions, including the feminine. The illusion that people are separate from their Source was no longer recognized to be an illusion, but became the principle message of all major religious thought. Power structures used the sublime utterances of those who had realized that Source and Seen were one in order to imply that they were *not* one. For example, the exquisite words attributed to Jesus Christ, "The kingdom of heaven is within you," have been used for thousands of years as part of a system towards an external future heaven!

These ideas of separation and the fear they naturally elicit were used to build powerful hierarchies. The beautiful idealisms of realizers like Christ and the Buddha were taught without any means for individuals to actualize these ideals in their everyday family life. The sense of the sacred was sequestered into a far-off realm, so that access could be mediated by those seeking power. Once you sell the public the idea of future idealism like Heaven, and persuade them they are born sinful, then you can convince them that you and your power structure can help them go 'beyond' or access God. It's a scam, an age-old get-rich-quick scheme. Convince people they are lacking and that you hold the solution. Take one look at the Vatican to see a vast concentration of wealth in the hands of a few, achieved through manipulating the public with the beautiful words of Jesus and selling access to that beauty as if everyone was not *the* beauty already. Religious practice became a disempowering search for God rather than an easy and egalitarian practice of participation in the Godliness of our very being.

Once it was believed that Source and Seen were two separate things, the method arose to try and reach the Source by denying the Seen. For example, it has been taught for millennia that the ultimate life involves going to the monastery or 'going within' through meditation for some 'higher' purpose, rather than the embrace of all ordinary conditions, including Sex. Much of the pain and confusion we feel around love, Sex, and relationships stems from this cultural legacy that has scorned the feminine—the body, other people, the world, and reality as it is experienced—in search of other 'higher' realities. The methods promoted by the world religions to discover these 'higher' places are renunciation and detachment. The religious power structures underpinning civilization moved us away from tangible experience and promoted 'abiding as witness only.' The weight of this cultural suggestion has turned the mind inward, away from relatedness and Sex, for the idea of some future attainment in consciousness or God. If you had not made the heroic gesture of going to the monastery—if you were still in the village having Sex and a family—you were less. Sex was less. Women were less. Both have for centuries been seen as worldly distractions, obstructions to God-realization or enlightenment. The promise of Buddhist or Christian monastic life is that if you detach from and abide as witness only to all arising conditions then you will come know God, Source, consciousness itself, the absolute, enlightenment, what-have-you. The so-called 'lesser' aspects of life—the material world, everyday life, food, money, women, Sex, birth, and death, which in the end *are* your whole life—are reduced to merely things to be 'aware' of. Or worse, they are presented as obstacles to your future spiritual realization. It is the stressed man meditating while his partner makes breakfast and anxiously tries to keep the children quiet; the young person who taps out of the difficulties of relationship and goes searching for inner peace in India; the mother who is made to feel like mothering is less than a proper job; the dissociative person, afraid to feel, who is attracted to the spiritual ideal of 'detachment' and not needing anyone; the 'spiritual teacher' convincing a follower that their grief at the loss of a loved one is mere 'worldly attachment.'

In promoting such distinctions, the world religions have put humanity in conflict with our own reality. Instead of embracing our lives, these cultures have promoted only the 'witnessing' of experience, which inherently is a project of dissociation. The mere fact that you are witnessing your experience implies that you are separate from it. Detachment as a practice has distracted humanity from enjoying our inherent connection to the natural state of the body and all its relatedness.

Humanity has had no idea what to do with the power and vulnerability of the feminine. Scared of this uncontrollable world of change, our predecessors attempted to control it or escape from it. Rather than participating peacefully in the great mystery of life and death, they created myths of eternity, hopes of transcendence, and castles of power and control. Religious and political institutions have furthered this fearful search for dominance over the living world, in the process abusing the Earth and controlling women. Their patriarchal doctrines have sunk deep into our collective psyche, dissociating us from the sublime regenerative force of life that it is our birthright to feel. Fear of death has resulted in fear of life, manifested as disconnection and numbness. Men have committed themselves to the male fantasy of their legacy and to their hope for continuity of identity after death, including the institutional continuity of what they were committed to in their lifetime. The search to 'abide as awareness,' 'go within,' 'know God beyond all conditions,' 'make a mark on the world,' or 'leave a legacy' is merely the desire to live forever, and the egoic identity around that idea. Man is missing out on a life committed to the tangible and to relationships with and within life. A hoax has been perpetrated suggesting that if we avoid all ordinary conditions and avoid receptivity we can find true power and mastery over this problematic world of change.

But power without receptivity is not really strong at all. Strength divorced from feeling-sensitivity to all life is destructive and brittle. It snaps easily. When we become strong but can't receive, we shut down our engagement with life, effectively fencing ourselves in. When you've been brought up from early childhood to be strong and to achieve but haven't learned receptivity, then by your twenties or thirties you may find yourself feeling bound and restricted—or nothing at all. The western cultural model has firmly implanted a need for success in most of us, whether in secular or spiritual pursuits. Our natural response has been to become rigid in the process. Strength of this kind destroys itself, degenerating into illness and manifesting as a feeling of being at war with life—with yourself and everything else. Real strength is able to receive and support life, rather than control or dominate it. Receptivity enables us to give ourselves to relationship and all its actual conditions, rather than avoid it for the idea of eternity. And then in relationship to actual life and its actual conditions we perceive eternity, presently arising as life.

So what we mean by patriarchy is not just an embattled sense of man versus woman, but a felt-sense of embattlement in all, as the cultural patterns of domination over nature and withdrawal from relatedness are felt within our own bodies. The movement away from ordinary conditions instilled in us by thousands of years of religious seeking *is* the denial of the feminine.

The womanless men of orthodoxy have been the leaders of our world for too long. Humanity continues to be obsessed with attempting to conquer or escape natural desires (or conversely, casually exaggerate and exploit them, still based on the belief that they are less than sacred). Man is still in conflict with his own reality, especially with Sex, and especially with woman and vice versa. From these beliefs we inherit the assumption that Sex is lesser or debased, and with this the burden of pornography and abuse. It is only now that misogyny is being revealed as the common behavior of humanity everywhere.

We must come back into horizontal relatedness with all ordinary conditions and feel the wonder that is already our lives. Real life is not a project to get somewhere as if you are not somewhere. We are deeply brainwashed to seek for spiritual ideals. It sneaks up on us in so many devious ways. It is like a virus that pervades the body. By understanding this intrusion and with radical release we can bloom in our own garden.

## The Union of Opposites

Though the religious idea that Source and Seen (or heaven and earth, male and female, form and spirit) are separate has gone into all of us, we have to admit that neither one can exist without its counterpart. If we think about it, we can clearly see that the universe is an impeccable union of opposites. Each opposite implies the other—left and right, front and back, above and below, inner and outer, inhale and exhale. Every atom in our body has a balance of opposing forces. This is all of life. And, as there is no right without left, no front without a back, earthly life cannot exist separate from its heavenly Source. In all living things, the union of opposites is in place from the very beginning.

Look at a tree. We see a powerful trunk rooted deeply to stand erect. It is hard and upright; the eternal strength of life. When we get up to the foliage, we see that it is soft and succulent. Every leaf is so juicy and wide open. Nutrients are received and collected for the health and well-being of all the trees. Their subtle chemistries are shared, transported by the power of life and the mysteries of soil and roots to ensure the continuity and improvement of all other trees. Without the foliage, the trunk would be stiff and eventually wither or rot. Without the magnificent trunk, there could be no foliage reaching toward the sunlight.

This is exactly how your wonder-full life is functioning. You have a masterful base and spine that support your soft crown and receptive front. Just like a tree you absorb light; you can't help it. All of life is this equation of 'strength receiving.' This is the nature of reality; the natural state of all things. Source and Seen *are* one. Just as the tree requires nothing extra to confirm its authenticity, neither do we. We both have a right to be here peacefully.

In our short lives here there is so much to perceive and receive. Life is a constant nurturing force. We are completely taken care of by nature. We are this union. Our flesh and blood, our heartbeat and breath and Sex, are the perfect intelligence of life. We are already manifesting God; we can't help it! The intelligent union of opposites exists in every cell of our bodies. The strength of the base of our body and the spine perfectly complements our soft, receptive front—an exquisite union which provides all that we need to receive and embrace our life. There is nowhere else we need to go, nothing else we need to be, and no way to get 'closer' to God. The very attempt to 'realize' God (or peace, or love) denies the divine perfection already appearing as you and me. The wholeness we seek under the name of God, Jehovah, Ishvara, Allah, Holy Father, Divine Mother, Jesus Christ, Shakti, Shiva, Io, Brahma, Great Spirit, Vishnu, Durga, Kali, Saraswati, Lakshmi, and a thousand other names is already present as us!

This means there is no approach to the divine and nothing to attain. God is there in our effortless participation in what is already given: the natural flow of life and energy that is the breath of the body, the pulse of heart, and the movement of Sex as a wholly positive and beautiful function of love.

I have spoken to many people who struggle to accept the religious dualisms that the great faiths are founded on. The idea that God is separate from humans, that heaven is separate from earth, that spirit is separate from matter, that the sacred is separate from the everyday, and that Sex is something to be hidden or denied, produces a deeply painful split in our lives. Our attention is diverted away from what really matters. Every day we are struck by the sheer wonder of the world around us and the gifts of ordinary life—the profundity of the body and the sacredness of Sex (a flower, for example, as the Sex of plants, or a ripe fruit). And yet our full embrace of what has been given is held back by the idea there is some higher state to attain. This may not be conscious, even. It's the vague feeling that we're not quite there yet; that we're not allowed to relax yet. That we don't belong in life and that we are somehow deeply flawed and not worth bothering with. These ideas create the struggle to attain a more spiritual life.

All the while, the highest reality we could wish for is available to us, as participation in the ever-present union of the heart's opposites, and in relatedness and all that flowers from it, including literal new life. It is here that the saints and sages of humanity dwell. Throughout history, there have been great thinkers and feelers who have affirmed the sacredness of all ordinary conditions. Rather than endorsing dissociative transcendence or renunciation, these few mystics throughout time have affirmed that Sex is indeed the heart's activity, caused and realized through the utter union of strength and receptivity (whether in same-sex or opposite-sex intimacy). But as the comedian Bill Hicks quipped, "We kill those people." Their religious establishments got rid of them, because the message that everyone can have their own direct relationship with Eternity in the midst of their current life is extremely destabilizing to those seeking to sell and control access to it. The idea of a future heaven has been used as a way to control the people's behavior in fear and paranoia, when all the while here we are in heaven!

Attempting to escape our dysfunctional social inheritance through the usual spiritual assumptions does not help—in fact, it makes matters worse, as it is the division of 'spiritual' and 'worldly' that has caused the dysfunction in the first place. The only spiritual process worth anything is the reunification of the masculine and feminine qualities of our own bodies and hearts. Or rather, participation in the perfect union that is already the case. Feeling this intimacy within, we immediately become capable of intimacy with another. The forces of male with female created the heart originally and abide now as the heart. This is our source, the absolute nurturing condition of reality. This is God. Nowhere else. God is not hiding somewhere. God-realization or enlightenment is a hoax perpetrated on a gullible public. There is no such thing! Only the heart of every life is God. This reunification is the primordial religion of humanity before patriarchy imposed its will on humanity. Only now do we begin to repair the cultural insanity that has dissociated us from our lived reality.

## What Goes Up Must Come Down (And What Goes Down Must Come Up)

In the orthodox religions, there has been an obsession with the idea of ascent. The sages of Europe were depicted with circles of light above their heads, called haloes, signifying subtle experiences above the crown and their ascension to higher states all the way to heaven. While subtle experiences above the crown are indeed possible, the valuation of them above all else created the assumption that what was below was less or even negative, an obstruction to the purity above. Monastic life was dedicated to the continuity of ascent and the denial of what was considered low or negative. But it was the idea of 'high' that created the idea of 'low.'

In religious sects of India, too, subtle ascending energies have been valued at the expense of everything else. Spiritual life was and is dedicated to sublimating the lower life—the lower chakras, for example—for the ascent to the beyond, and even out of the body. Vast cultures have been created on this male fantasy of ascent or enlightenment.

But I have to tell you, there is no stable ascent without descent. In our lives, there is both ascent and descent; they are two synchronistic merging activities of opposites in union, like everything else. For a sage to ascend and become stable in that ascent, she or he must first descend. We must primarily receive. We can express this with another or feel it within our own forms. It is not a matter of sublimating or denying the lower, but honoring what is so-called 'low' and what is horizontal in the related conditions. This is the very means of saintly ascent, where should we ascend in our subtle energies, it is in the context of prior and synchronistic receptivity.

In some pockets of ancient India and other indigenous cultures, the whole body of the sage was effulgent. All directions were felt to be full of light. High did not imply anything negative about low. Subtle did not imply anything negative about gross. (God did not imply anything negative about Sex!) When you turn out into all conditions everywhere and participate in what is already happening in Mother Nature and in the body, there is a full radiance, a whole-body halo, not just a concentration in or above the head. All conditions are embraced in that radiance. We are not here only to try and get out of here. But there are so many examples of sages who are, in fact, life denying. They are glamourizing subtle conditions, subtle energies, or just the idea of consciousness that is transcendent of all tangible conditions. This attainment is presented as the goal, either explicitly or by their example. A certain lightness of being may make them attractive to their devotees. This dissociative phenomenon has been branded into the human psyche as what life's all about. It wreaks havoc on the lives of all who try to follow it, as they attempt to discard all their tangible life conditions, their relationships, and their prior responsibility to engage sexual intimacy with utter positivity. Unless sexuality is worked out, it comes out as an illness later, no matter what the conditions of ascent.

In my early life, I was seduced by a number of saints and sages in India and around the world. I am delighted to have met their luminosity, beauty, and friendship, yet many of their lives and teachings denied for myself and others full embrace and participation in all tangible conditions. I was astonished to find that across the world's wonderful teachings, there was no link made between the spiritual realization being offered and the very real needs of people to engage relationship and Sex. And I don't mean vulgar technique-driven exaggeration or the search for novelty experiences through the medium of another person. I learnt that the lives and teachings of great saints and sages must be put into the context of the message of this book: that God and Sex are indeed one. The embrace of all tangible conditions *is* the embrace of God. When we give up the search for God or ascent, we are not giving up the possibility of sublime inspiration. I would even say that the luminosity of the saints and sages I have met and my relationship with them has only been fruitful through my embrace of intimacy with every aspect of life.

## CHAPTER THREE

# *The Hoax of Enlightenment*

*I see us hew great mountains down*
*I see us in a lovely place*
*I see us naked of lies together*
*I see us naked of disgrace*
*I see trust born in us through honour*
*And I see peace come*
*And if I don't get it wrong*
*I see us all get home.*

—Robin Williamson, 'I See Us All Get Home'

ENLIGHTENMENT IS A MALE FANTASY. IT IS A HOAX IMPOSED ON humanity. The attempt to get somewhere sublime or extraordinary, as if you are not already the extraordinary wonder of reality, has itself created the complex avoidance of relationship that is now the normal behavior within all societies. It is the denial of life in the name of 'higher' realities.

This model of hierarchical ascendance has given power to false authorities of all kinds—kings, popes, priests, teachers and gurus—to establish delusional systems in which they manipulate others. It is usually accompanied with the denial of Sex, because progress up these fabricated hierarchies always involves a conquering of our natural desires and the natural need for relationship. A Catholic priest once said to me, "We've gone the extra mile because we've given up Sex." Such teachings underpin our social inequalities of male and female and have created the vast fabric of sexual dysfunction that we see all around us. Well-meaning parents have for generations filled their children with shame around sexuality and their body in the sincere belief they were helping them become 'better' or more moral human beings. Teachers and parents have really believed that by suppressing and controlling sexuality they were doing us a favor, when in reality they were setting us up for misery. I recently met a woman who was told by her teacher, whom she loved, that if she masturbated then her mother would die. As a young girl, she believed this! It takes years to undo the deep shame around Sex created by this kind of delusion. And yet the teacher probably sincerely believed she was helping this young girl be closer to God. She herself was most likely deeply suppressed in her sexuality and relational life, and was just passing on the shoddy goods she had received from prior authorities. Every one of them was deprived. We do not need their methods in order to become more pure or holy and progress up the hidden hierarchy towards God.

The pursuit of enlightenment is the original self-improvement scam. The model of the perfect person, the 'enlightened' one, implies that you and everyone else are not perfect and not yet enlightened. It is the social dynamic of disempowerment, whereby someone may imagine they are 'finished' or an 'advanced practitioner' or 'just a beginner' in the random criteria by which people measure themselves as winners and losers—mostly losers. The mere assumption of someone being finished or advanced makes everyone feel less. The idea that someone is in a special state and we are not keeps our attention away from the miracle that is our very existence.

Renunciate organizations led by self-proclaimed 'enlightened' gurus seduce sincere people into the paradigm of linear ascendance to God, where one is either progressing or regressing towards or away from enlightenment—often known as 'overcoming one's ego.' Under the authority and charm of the perfect person, people undertake the hero's journey toward this mythical state, traditionally measured by a variety of different feats of life-denial: sitting all day in meditation, not talking to other people, fasting, throwing out most of your clothes, falling out of society, not having Sex, having a lot of exaggerated sex without feeling any emotion, living in a cave, or effortfully trying to not feel any sort of 'attachment' to anything or anyone. These traditions are gilded with mythological stories of mostly male heroes who are perceived to have reached the goal. The teacher is enamored by the attention of the audience. It makes them feel really good about themselves, and they become radiant and attractive like a Mick Jagger on stage, made seemingly happy and appealing by the attention of their audience. People who establish themselves as enlightened teachers are often fearful personalities who make their claim in order to anxiously control their social circumstance. First you have to fool yourself before you fool the people.

If you are someone who has fallen in love with such a figure, your love is to be honored, and your sincere impulse is beautiful. But beware of the social dynamic of disempowerment, and the idea that you have to get somewhere as if you are not somewhere. The notion of having to do anything to improve ourselves or to get to some better state is itself the problem that prevents us from enjoying the fullness and the profundity of what and where we are.

There are those of our modern time who say that they are not gurus and that they are the same as everyone else, yet they maintain their special behaviors, special outfits, and special social status (and income, *et cetera*). They are still not relating in an ordinary way with other people, and often blame their followers for putting them on the pedestal that they are meanwhile literally sitting upon and could get off at any time. This is a particularly convoluted and confusing arrangement for participants. I'm sure Jesus wouldn't have done this and would have been a genuine friend. A teacher is no more than a friend, no less than a friend, the function of nurturing in local community.

As the author of this book, there is nothing truly important that I know that you don't know. The knowing is already alive *as* us. Our bodies are the intelligence of nature. Our hair grows and our hearts beat without us having to think about it. If you, as an organism, didn't already know everything you need to know to be a human, you would be dead. Your heart is already open. If it wasn't, you'd be dead. Life is already looking after us perfectly well. The magnificence of life does not await you, it actually IS you. Beware anyone who tries to convince you that enlightenment is the goal, however charming and powerful they may be. You are already a body of light, in prior relationship with light, pervaded by it and in perfect harmony with it. There is no need to search for enlightenment. You can relax.

## CHAPTER FOUR

# *The Medieval Chain of Being*

*Religious dreams and holy vespers light thy smoky fires:*
*Once were thy fires lighted by the eyes of honest morn.*
—William Blake, *Visions of the Daughters of Albion*

We live still in the ruins and remains of the medieval 'Great Chain of Being,' a deluded order of human privilege and poverty that gripped Europe for many centuries and was spread around the world by colonialism. This thought structure defined all of life within a vast hierarchy, from God, the king, and the aristocracy and clergy, down through professionals, traders, and peasants, through to animals (the most reviled of which were snakes, for their bad behavior in the Garden of Eden), plants, and minerals. The natural interdependence and wonder of all life was denied by this hierarchical order, within which each category of beings was seen as a link in the divinely ordered chain, unable to move up or down. The classes below were abused; the classes above obeyed. Men were believed to be inherently superior to women. This wasn't recognized as a belief system; it merely seemed like 'how it is,' the perfect order of things as ordained by God. And we should note that it wasn't an arbitrary philosophy: it served the specific material interests of those at the top of the pile. Anyone seeking to usurp the hierarchy or point out its gross injustice could be accused of blasphemy (disobedience to God). Wealth flowed upwards and abuse flowed downwards.

Within the Great Chain of Being, the human being is caught in the middle ground, sharing some traits with the angels and Gods above and others with the animals, plants, and mere terrestrial entities below. Higher status is associated with transcendence of the body and of Sex. Because women were associated with the earthly aspect, they were a lower link on the chain. It was this ideology that suppressed woman and restricted them from the priesthood. Man was associated with God and woman with Sex, and never the twain shall meet—except to procreate and produce more men to preach the doctrine or go to war for it. Because of the imaginary split, women were believed to be incapable of relating to God and should therefore content themselves with serving men, who would serve God for them. In *Paradise Lost* (1667), John Milton betrayed his misogynist bias in famous words describing Adam and Eve: "He for God only, She for God in him." Milton's poetic genius unwittingly summarized the religious misogyny originating in the Abrahamic traditions in these few pithy words, a testament to his artistry. It is this ideology that reigns still in many religious societies today, rendering women, the body, and Sex lesser, taboo, and highly controlled. And reigns still to some degree in secular life, where the man serves career and status and the woman serves the man. If man would look to God in women, then we'd all get home.

Look at how the philosophy of the Chain of Being served specific interests: the king was believed to be sanctioned by God as the 'head of state,' the source of truth and authority, whereas the peasant masses were the lesser, exploited 'body' of the kingdom. The 'head of state' was a tyrant who ruled the body politic, just as the father of each family, having adopted this patriarchal patterning, tended to be the tyrannical authority of the home—the 'head of the household.' This logic of dominance from the macrocosm to the microcosm was made explicit by the monarchs themselves:

> In the Scriptures kings are called Gods, and so their power after a certain relation compared to the Divine power. Kings are also compared to fathers of families; for a king is truly *parens patriae* [parent

> of the country], the politic father of his people. And lastly, kings are compared to the head of this microcosm of the body of man."
>
> —James I of England, from a speech to Parliament in 1610.

Meditation, celibacy, renunciation, transcendence of desire, and the suppression of our 'animal' instincts all imply the logic of this ancient hierarchy in their attempt to deny embodiment and partnership and move towards God. Whether we are medieval people programmed to humbly accept our place in the chain, or modern people programmed to aggressively try and work our way up it, the imaginary hierarchy remains. And of course the form is not limited to Europe. Eastern religions and cultural systems have their own versions of the chain, for example the Buddhist hierarchies of evolving and improving reincarnations towards the ultimate goal of leaving the earth completely. Spiritual enlightenment (release from the cycles of birth and death) is presented as the grand prize atop this variation on the Chain of Being. But while God is still believed to be at the top, we will never know God.

In our own bodies, the uninvestigated thought structures of our 'head' rule still as a false tyrant over the sublimity of our own body, which is already in perfect harmony with the rest of existence. Just as the king denied his utter dependence on the functional body-politic that grew his food and sustained him, so does our own head deny its utter dependence on the natural body and life that it arises as a function of. We are not the king/head controlling a body; we are the whole body, whatever the miracle and mystery of the body actually is. The body was perfectly peaceful until we went looking for peace and power at the top of the Chain.

We can now see that the entire structure was a Ponzi scheme*, a means of wealth accumulation. Nothing can be second to anyone or anything or superior to anyone or anything. Life doesn't come in a hierarchy. It is all just happening.

---

* Ponzi scheme: a form of fraud in which belief in the success of a non-existent enterprise is fostered by the payment of quick returns to the first investors from money invested by later investors.

# CHAPTER FIVE

## *What is Going On Here?*

*It's always easier not to think for oneself. Find a nice safe hierarchy and settle in. Don't make changes, don't risk disapproval... It's always easiest to let yourself be governed.*

—Ursula K. Le Guin, *The Dispossessed*

MANY OF US WERE RAISED IN RELIGIOUS FAMILIES AND HAVE SEEN first-hand the kind of disempowerment that takes place when God is conceived of as the head of a divine hierarchy operating in a distant realm. Across the world, powerful men high up within the hierarchies teach and practice misogyny. Women are still taught that they are second to men and that women's independence of mind and sexuality is lesser. Men are still deprived of the feminine and enacting their repressed sexuality in secretive abuse. We may have grown up going to church, reading religious literature and partaking in religious practice, and everywhere we looked it was only (or mostly) men who were wearing the robes and speaking the gospel. And we thought: what the hell is going on here?

We intuitively understand that women and men are intrinsically equal and we experience gender equality in some other parts of our lives—whether it be in our own families and relationships, in our community and workplaces, or in the wider political life of our country. Yet when it comes to spiritual life, women are still seen as less. Some are able to pick and choose parts of the religious teachings and leave out other parts. Fair enough. Others cannot accept the co-option of the great wisdom traditions of humanity by patriarchal power structures.

When we look a little deeper, we find that it is not just that actual women are seen as less by religious institutions. It is the principle of the feminine itself, which is then associated with actual women as a way for powerful men to dissociate from it. First, the principles of masculine (God) and feminine (Sex) are believed to be separate; then the former is seen as superior to the latter; then men are associated with the former (priesthood, agency, moral authority, spirit, power) and women with the latter (reproduction, earthly, worldly, shallow, emotional, messy). We can scarcely speak about this process of divide and conquer, such is the valid outrage many feel at having been put in these limiting boxes where only half of their humanity is permitted. The artificial divisions are riddled with contradictions, such as the requirement for women to be both sexually 'pure' (the virgin) and sexually available (the whore). Or the belief that women are both sexually passive (no autonomous desire) and sexually ravenous (needing to be controlled). These expectations are united in seeing the feminine as an object, rather than a subject. (The very fact that the feminine has been so obsessively controlled is testament to its power and vitality.) When we assume God and Sex are separate and that God is elsewhere, then the feminine and all of material reality can be used and abused as mere utilitarian object. The philosophy that says women can't be priests is the same thought pattern underpinning the abuse of women and the earth. The treatment of women is indicative of a deeper problem.

The attempt to dissociate from the feminine also leads to the denial of sexuality and embodiment within each individual. Young men who want to serve their communities and do good are seduced by religious persuasions and have their life taken from them. They are taught that to get to God they must give up Sex and women, and are in some cases literally deprived of their mothers and contact with women. This results in an all-pervasive pathology in this world and filters down to the denial of life and abusive behaviors in general society. When God and Sex are separated, both are toxified.

The beautiful spiritual ideals promoted by priests of all kinds and which the faithful find sincere inspiration in stand in stark contrast to the reality of misogyny, homophobia, and sexual violence that is rife across all temple religions. The exquisite texts of the world's great religions—the Quran, the Bhagavad Gita, the Guru Granth Sahib, the Bible, the Talmud, the Buddhist Sutras—are treasures of ancient and modern wisdom culture. We hold these texts close to our hearts, irrespective of how they may have been misused. The teaching of Christ to "Love thy neighbor as thyself" is an attractive ideal that we cannot argue with. Yet how can we reconcile the teachings of Christ with the behavior of Catholic priests? How can we continue to trust or endorse the temple religions who speak one way and act another?

Ultimately, the very construction of a hierarchical organization where some people claim exclusive access to God robs everyone else of their intrinsic relationship with God and presents the church as the gatekeeper and arbiter of God's love. The proposition that a relationship with God can be hoarded and policed and the idea that certain people are closer to God than others makes everyone else feel less. It is still the Chain of Being, and such hierarchy has no place within spiritual life.

I was recently walking around in Thailand in a field filled with enormous looming Buddha statues. Male monks were worshipping at the statues, while all the women and children were sneaking around these dark foreboding forms, fearful that some all-powerful figure could redeem or destroy their lives at any moment. Everywhere I went I saw these giant statues. They reminded me of the foreboding gothic towers of Europe in all their grim beauty, beneath which the people went about their lives fearfully stooped. Within the context of disempowerment, powerful religious figures use their standing in the community and the glamorous architecture of their religion to make everyone paranoid. It is only now that we are beginning to see the respectable edifices crack.

We are grateful to so many known and unknown religious pioneers who questioned the oppression within their own faith and spoke their own experience clearly. One example is the Italian friar and philosopher Giordano Bruno (1548–1600), who declared that each person could have their own direct relationship with God, which did not need to be mediated by church or state. This was such a threat to the church that they burned him in the public square. A statue acknowledges him in Rome to this day. Religion has always been filled with women and men like Bruno, who spoke up for direct participation in what Life is and were tortured or killed for it. The narratives of religion we have inherited are those of the power holders, but every religion has a rich history of dissent, renewal, remodeling, and authentic expression. And we are grateful to Johannes Gutenberg (1400–1468) of Mainz, Germany, who changed the world forever with his invention of the printing press and production of the first printed book in 1455, a Bible. Prior to this, religious texts were handwritten by priests of orthodoxy, the power holders of the church. Gutenberg paved the way for ordinary people to have access to sacred text, so they could check it out and interpret it for themselves. They could then participate in the shaping of ideas in further world-changing printed texts such as Martin Luther's *95 Theses.* This process continues to this day, where the masses of humanity hold smartphones and have immediate access to every form of information. I consider the present book to be part of this process. The process is gradual by which we learn to make intelligent use of the information in our hands. We need no longer allow our relationship with life to be mediated by power holders.

CHAPTER SIX

# *Religion Made Useful*

*Spirit means breath, that is the Latin definition of the word. Nothing more, Sir!*

—U.G. Krishnamurti

RELIGION BECOMES USEFUL AND TRUE AS THE PATRIARCHAL IDEAS of separation and hierarchy dissolve. Whether it is the temple faithful of Hinduism and Buddhism; or the world faiths of Islam, Christianity, Judaism, and all their derivatives; or the many sincere faithful people of Sikhism, Jainism, Zoroastrianism, Ba'hai, and all the other rich articulations of faith, every religious individual requires a way to directly embrace the radiance of their own condition. Without the practical means to *participate* in your faith, religion becomes a socially prescribed search for God,* as if God is absent. The thought structures that place God in heaven and humans on Earth and promote some kind of arbitrary project to 'get back' to God and know source obliterate our ability to perceive that we are God! They prevent us from honoring our own mother as the divine mother, who formed the cells of our body from her own.

---

* Or sublimity, the void, pure emptiness, ultimate liberation, or enlightenment, as the case may be within non-theistic religions.

We must urgently put a practice of intimacy with all tangible conditions into our daily lives so that we can live unqualified by the limitations of patriarchal power structures. We need a practical and personal means of participating in our own Godhood, in the Godliness of all existing conditions, and in the sacredness of our chosen deities (which are symbolic personifications of the power of Life, not the sole location of it), so we can remove ourselves from the superstitious cultism of temple religion.

The poetry and power of the great religious texts have been used to hold our ordinary lives ransom for thousands of years. The sublimity of the idea of heaven casts a shadow over Earth. And the beautiful ideals of spiritual life promoted by the temple religions, such as 'love thy neighbor as thyself,' often stand in stark contrast to our daily lives and interactions. Without the practical means to embrace the profundity of our lives, these principles remain ideals only, comforting concepts. A future promise that exists only as a nice idea in the mind. In fact, sublime teachings without the practical means to actualize these ideals makes our lives worse. We are left with a sense of failure as our deep social obstructive patterns, fears, and trauma prevent our ideals being implemented despite our best intentions. We are stuck appealing to a higher power to save us, like a drowning person with their arms waving above their head begging for help, when all they had to do was lower their arms and start swimming and the shore was twenty yards away. And some of us have very beautiful, very sophisticated, very intoxicating ways of appealing for help. There's so much beauty in it and so much charm and cadence in the priests and gurus. But no one is coming to save us, no matter how nicely or desperately we wave our arms. Appealing to higher powers keeps us helplessly lower. We change from temple religions of appeal to participatory religion in God, reality itself, in relationship with all things. This is not to criticize anyone, just to lay out our options: do you want to drown or do you want to swim? Either way, you're in the water.

The daily embrace of our body and breath is known as the mother's milk of spiritual life. Conscious moving and breathing is the literal enactment of giving and receiving, which is the basis of all life. In the giving of life there is immediate and synchronistic receiving of life. In the receiving of life there is the synchronistic ability to give life. This is how reality is functioning, how life creates and sustains all forms, the male-female power and polarity of the natural state. Through daily practice, your ability to be intimate strengthens. It is like working a muscle. We can then extend our intimacy to our neighbor in a very natural way. Through intimacy with the breath, we notice that we are part of Life and are then able to love ourselves. It then becomes practically possible to 'love our neighbor as ourselves.' Without knowing ourselves as part of things, we can't love ourselves and so can't love our neighbor. When we throw out the idea that we are not there yet, the parables, sutras, fables, and commandments stop being unattainable ideals that turn us into hypocrites and become real and ordinary, at once sublime and prosaic.

As the primary separation between tangible life and the spiritual or the heavenly is *felt* to be untrue by the whole body, all other divisions that are dependent on this assumption also disappear. The divisions dissolve in which *some* things are sacred and some things are not: some people sacred and others not, some places and moments sacred and others not, God sacred and Sex not. The desire for something sacred in our life is a beautiful desire, but it must include everything. Spirit is not an abstraction. Not something inside. Not something outside. Not something above. Not something other. Spirit is the living body, whatever the body is altogether in all its intrinsic relatedness and all its dimensions above and below. Body and mind's participation in Sex *is* participation in spirit, the power and movement of reality itself.

Religion is founded around great human beings—Buddha, Christ, and Mohammed, for example—who realized that hierarchies did not exist, but whose beautiful words were then co-opted to build hierarchies. In throwing out the hierarchies, we do not need throw out our relationship with these realizers. We can hold the baby and drain the bathwater.

Yet it can be a lonely experience to step out of these divisive thought structures, because all conventional institutions and behaviors in our world are based on separation and fear. Our enthusiastic participation in the downtown church may diminish, and we may lose interest in conventional aggressive politics or career. We are disheartened to see the injustice imposed on many and the disempowerment of people created by the hoped-for greatness of doctrine that implies a present inadequacy. But if we have the courage to stand alone, we find that we stand with the whole. I exist because everything else exists and it is obvious.

Paradoxically, this insight may give us the strength to stay inside our social or religious institutions if we choose. We may have issues with thought and social structures, but ultimately not with people, because it is all Life happening. We may find that we can engage with the religious traditions of our family and the community with a new lightness. We can go to Sunday service, we can fast during Ramadan, we can make holy pilgrimage and offer prayer with our parents, and we can do so safe in the knowledge that the wonder of our life and our relationship to our faith is unbounded by the perversions, hierarchies, dogma and misogyny of the power structures that have manipulated the public in the name of God for thousands of years. We are not gullible children believing in a parental authority figure, but neither are we in adolescent conflict with them. We reconnect with the essential beauty and power of religious utterance.

I would like to purify Sex in all religious traditions, so their participants are no longer in conflict with their born experience and may participate in Sex and all tangible conditions as their very communion with their chosen deity. And I would like the same for those traditions who do not have the God concept but do practice reverence for Life, the absolute condition of Life. No one need be in conflict with any naturally occurring phenomena of Life, but should be free to participate in them with absolute positive connection to everything.

This book is here to purify and heal these words: God, Sex, and Religion. Religion is made useful when we engage it in the truest sense of the word: to relink. We relink our minds to their source, which is heart, arising as every thing. Whether we choose to call it God or not, this is the sublimity. Now, we can practice all our religious cultural forms happily.

CHAPTER SEVEN

# *God, Sex, and Science*

*The Dark religions are departed and sweet science reigns.*

— William Blake, *Vala, or the Four Zoas*

*His face is turned toward the past. Where we perceive a chain of events, he sees one single catastrophe which keeps piling wreckage upon wreckage and hurls it in front of his feet. The angel would like to stay, awaken the dead, and make whole what has been smashed. But a storm is blowing from Paradise; it has got caught in his wings with such violence that the angel can no longer close them. The storm irresistibly propels him into the future to which his back his turned, while the pile of debris before him grows skyward. The storm is what we call progress.*

—Walter Benjamin, *Angelus Novus*, or *The Angel of History*

AT THIS JUNCTURE, SOME OF YOU MAY BE THINKING, "What's this got to do with me, I'm not a religious person; I'm a modern person who doesn't believe in any of that." I'm sorry to say that religious or no, the thought structures and behaviors of the society you were born into* have been formed by its religious history and are still active. By

* Excepting a very few pockets of off-the-grid indigenous societies around the world.

understanding the continuity of thought from past to present, we can understand our own tendencies of thought and not be limited by them.

The reason we may believe ourselves to be unaffected is that the period in western thought known as 'the Scientific Revolution' or the 'Enlightenment' is often seen as the birth of a bold new era of Reason, an absolute break with the superstitions of the past. Within the master narratives of culture, the 'Enlightenment' is looked to as the point where society rejected the medieval Chain of Being and rid itself of the mystifying thought structures of temple religion. There is a great deal of inherited cultural pride around this history. But the bad news is that it was not a clean break. We managed to *inherit and repurpose* the dualisms of the religious model without questioning their perspective on nature, Sex, and the body. The priesthood of religion handed over the robes to the priesthood of science. Although their battle continues to the present day, it is the invisible assumptions they share that we should be concerned about, not their differences. From superstitious past to rational present, we still imagine ourselves to be separate from experience, from each other, and from Life itself. Our body and nature is still seen as dumbed down materiality, something less than God, that we as a supposedly separate mind (or soul) can consume and exploit, drug and manipulate.

Europe's Scientific Revolution or 'Age of Reason' absolutely did see new thinking undermine some of the harmful superstitious ideas of temple religion—the belief in witches, for example, or a myriad of other harmful beliefs in heavens, hells, and priestly mystifications. We are grateful for the shift in culture away from superstition that allows us to have this conversation, even. If you were caught reading this book in England in 1650, you would probably find yourself locked away, tortured, or burnt at the stake. Many people sacrificed their lives to give us the more accurate perspective on material mechanics that we now enjoy. In 1609, Johan Kepler upset people when he used mathematics to prove that the planets revolve around the sun rather than the earth (an idea first suggested by Polish monk Copernicus in 1543). In the same year, Galileo confirmed this view using observations made with the newly invented telescope. The compounding evidence upset man's assumption that he was the center of the universe, and also challenged the orthodox belief that the earth was made of different and inferior material than the supposedly perfect, unchanging celestial planets. Even the idea of above and below started to feel unstable. For the first time in European history (since written record keeping, at least), someone had noticed that the heavens 'above' were made of the same stuff as the earth 'below': rocks, craters, mountains, and gases. These observations were so destabilizing to religious doctrine that the Catholic church banned ideas of heliocentrism (sun as the center of the universe) as heresy and in 1633 imprisoned Galileo for the rest of his life. These great seekers after knowledge did much to bring us 'down to earth,' and we are grateful. The great destabilizations of the scientific revolution represent a shift of attention away from heavenly futures and abstract ideals and toward tangible material reality. Despite ongoing repression from religious states, there was an explosion of knowledge about the body and its functions, the natural world, causes of disease, and the principles of physical existence that enabled the invention of complex machinery. All of our modern sciences were forged during this period, as was the scientific method itself—empirical research, close observation, and the ideal of objectivity. Because so many of the new inventions and theories (such as Isaac Newton's theories of gravity and motion and research into the workings of light and color) directly contradicted religious perspectives taken to be the fabric of reality, the church lost power to control how people thought. Many volumes have been written on this major shift, so it's enough to say here that a new world was being built against religious mystification and the divine right of kings—a world in which the laws of profit and universal exchange would come to rule. Europe (and North America) saw waves of revolutionary upheaval and crises that broke the coupling of church and state. The scientific worldview had an advantage in the battle of thought, as it allied itself with these growing market societies and the desire to create profit through increased control of people and the natural world. These developments required a human-centric philosophy—an understanding that, even if one was religious (Newton, for example, still believed in a holy Creator), it was humanity's birthright to decipher, master, and control the universe. Under the new 'rational' paradigm, it was gradually admitted that God (as an abstraction or 'other') was not empirically provable, and was therefore questionable at best, fictional at worst. "God is dead!" the philosopher Nietzsche famously declared. The medieval Chain of Being was amended: no longer beholden to the 'divinely sanctioned' authority of the priesthood, humanity believed itself to now be the master of its own fate.

But humanity still had not actually come into relationship with the tangible reality that it was now so eagerly studying. Where once the earthly and physical was seen to be a lesser realm to be transcended, now it was a lesser realm to be investigated, controlled, observed, categorized, manipulated—and profited from. The underlying assumptions were really not all that different. Far from a clean break with religious thought structures, the scientific mind that thankfully arose from figures such as Galileo and the brave pioneers of modernity was a counterpose that arose in reaction to what had gone before (the assumption that God was 'other' and heaven was separate from and better than the earth). The same assumption prevailed: that humanity was separate from what it observed, whether viewing life as God's creation or through the microscope. The posture of science presumes the observer's separation. We are so used to this sense of distance that we are hardly aware it is a specific mode of perception, one that is useful as a temporary position while gathering empirical data, but not as the new religion. Not as a way to live.

In fact, the new priests of reason, lords of the rising industrial society, *embraced* the religious denial of the tangible/nature. They elevated the function of human reason to fill the place of God—still imagined as a transcendent force separate and superior to the material world of change, life, the body, death, birth and Sex. This ideology gave a God-like sense of ownership and entitlement, through the self-promotion of The Reasonable Man as the only intelligent form of life on Earth. Humankind still did not have the ability to be ardently connected to its own wonder. Reason was the new God, and some things had it, and some things did not. Sex was still less. Women were still less. The old/new denial was used to justify the exploitation of indigenous peoples, the natural world, women, the working-class, the body, and animals. If reason was the most valued (divine) faculty, then anything assumed not to possess reason could be objectified and owned. The philosopher René Descartes, for example, justified the exploitation of animals on the grounds that they lacked the essential faculty (reason) that would make their suffering genuine. Or, as the eighteenth-century writer Mary Wollstonecraft* wrote: "In what does man's pre-eminence over the brute creation, consist? The answer is as clear as that a half is less than a whole, in Reason." Ruling classes across Europe developed a new ideology of racism aligning African people with nature (Sex) rather than reason (God) in a strategic attempt to justify colonialism and slavery. The exploitation of workers in what English mystic William Blake (1757–1827) called the "satanic mills" of industrializing Europe relied on the same hierarchy, where the working class were seen as a mindless physical resource to be used and abused—certainly not as the undefinable beauty of life embodied in each person.

Life remained compartmentalized into a passive, instrumentalized material below and a separate 'director,' known as intelligence, mind, or reason above, with only this director seen to have vitality and agency. The dynamics of possessor and possessed continued, both within each person's body, within social relationships, and within the human relationship with the non-human natural world.

## The Fallout

Ancient religions proposed an autocratic super-intelligence pulling strings from somewhere else, essentially negating life's present intelligence, but contemporary science proposes a mechanical, knowable world that humanity can somehow master or control. It is an assumption that turns the world into a bland place, creating our separation as mere observers and isolating us from wonder. So, as modern people we may have become interested in our material conditions, but we have still not learned how to embrace our tangible reality in all its depth and mystery. The mechanistic account of the world inherited from

* As a pioneering feminist, Mary Wollstonecraft (1759–1797) sought to improve the

the scientific revolution obscures mystery in exchange for the goal of mastery. Clearly, these assumptions are not valid, but they have hurt us, leaving us searching for a depth of meaning that has never been absent. Reductive materialism dictates the ways in which we are able to think and express ourselves. It limits what is seen as credible to a very narrow form of instrumentalized reason. We feel this as a distance, a loss of intimacy with nature. Even if we believe that we 'love' nature, it remains a resource, something we go walking in for a 'fix' as if it is a separate, consumable experience rather than our own bodies. In reality, wherever we are we are in nature. That's what the sciences of biology and ecology have shown us. You can't get out of it!

We were born into a social environment that fills us with these absurd assumptions that alienate us from our natural state. This alienation has become so severe it is threatening our continued existence. At a planetary scale, the alliance between commerce and the unreconstructed religious dualisms of modernity has brought us to the brink of ecological collapse. Nature's body is hurting. As my friend Andy Raba writes:

> The planet has been dug up by minds who—where paradise spreads forth—see nothing but instruments of profit: Animals become Livestock, Trees become Logs, People become Slaves or Masters, Abundance is ransacked and hoarded. The paradox of our time is that the very technologies and forces that have brought us to ecological collapse are the same forces that could be directed towards a society of pleasure, luxury, shelter, wealth, food, clean drinking water, and freedom for every single human being.

From its basis in the dualistic split between mind and matter, modern culture rewrites the religious project of enlightenment into a project of mastery, manipulation, and domination of the body and of nature. Every one of us is affected by the inherited belief in a division between reason and nature; in fact the hallmark feature of modern secular

---

situation for women by proving that they too were reasonable beings, equally capable of ruling over 'brute creation,' rather than to undermine the arbitrary criteria of these hierarchies altogether.

society is the imagined split between mind (reason) and body (nature). The religious ideology of the warring forces of soul over the carnal body was effortlessly translated to the ideology of mind over unruly body. A host of features are allied to either side of the dualism, with the body and Sex coming off worse. As philosopher Val Plumwood writes,

> The main function of the concept of rationality, which has a confusing army of senses in which it is often hard to discern any precise content, seems to be a self-congratulatory one for the group thought to possess the prized quality and the exclusion and denigration of the contrasting group which does not. Thus the sphere of rationality variously contrasts with and excludes the sphere of emotions, the body, the passions, nature, the non-human world, faith, matter and physicality, experience and madness.

Look at the qualities that have been attached to the body/nature side of the duality. It is obvious how this thinking is the basis of patriarchal ideology. Centuries of control over women have been justified by associating them with the unruly qualities of nature and men with the qualities of reason. Women are seen as closer to nature: more embodied, more emotional, less rational, and more passive/immersed in the inevitable cycles of reproduction, birth, Sex and death. Harder to control, and therefore less. Many women alive today grew up being told they were incapable of the rational thought necessary to succeed at mathematics and physics, for example. By contrast, male dominance in public life relies upon their supposed separation from these 'feminine' traits—celebrating a sense of masculine rationality, control, objectivity, and lack of emotion. This definition of masculinity has been upheld as the ideal human model, whether it is believed that women are intrinsically 'different' and unable to attain it, or that they may aspire towards it, Margaret Thatcher style. The ideal human is therefore the Reasonable Man, as humans are supposedly differentiated from nature on the grounds of rationality. This is what is meant by patriarchy—the association of the qualities of freedom, control, transcendence, rationality, suppression of emotion, and courage with masculinity; and the association of immersion, passivity, Sex, birth, and death with the feminine. And the idea that the latter is lesser, and to be conquered. These ideas hurt both men and women. Men are deprived of the feminine, which is their birthright. They learn to suppress their feelings, and it creates depression, degenerative illness, and suicide. Women are denied their own power and life in the unhappy dominance of the male. This is what we have inherited and can purify now.

Think about how when women do break into the male-dominated spheres of politics and economics, the way in which they are received is policed by contradictory desires for how they should behave: female politicians' voices are often described as 'shrill' (meaning too emotional/not rational); on the other hand they are criticized for not being womanly enough if they do not smile and be nice to everyone. Or consider how within heated discussion, emotions are seen as less valid than cool, reasonable debate—even if the apparent rationality is cold, dissociative, unempathetic, and masking a dysfunctional inability to feel. I'm sure you've been told to 'be reasonable!' while trying to authentically express a feeling. Or been told that an expression of emotion is feminine and weak. Or learned to restrain the natural vulnerable expressions of emotion and pretend not to feel, in order to appear more rational or professional. Or tried to convince someone to change using factual argument, as if we are reasonable beings, rather than feeling ones. Or shamefully sought to conceal and control the natural processes of life such as menstruation or aging.

Within the framework that divides God from Sex, the mind from the body, reason from nature, everyone loses. The full spectrum of innate human functions—everything that has historically been classed as masculine and feminine—exists within each one of us. Happiness and health arise when all functions are permitted to express themselves fully in each person in their own unique combination. In free expression, these traits can be seen to mutually support one another. Consider how strength that is not receptive becomes brittle and self-destructive; how rationality without emotion quickly loses touch with the world; how our sense of freedom and control becomes dangerous when it is not coupled with an acceptance of our place within nature; or how courage without immersion becomes escapism and avoidance. By dividing up human faculties and prioritizing certain ones over others, the natural fulsome expression of each human being is obstructed and we become a risk to ourselves, others, and the planet. The whole mess of culture, religion, art, and science is the constant aberrant attempt to get back to feel again what was never lost. And all the while, the living radiance that is our breathing bodies, our relationships, the suffering Earth, and all of the beauty that is actual life is always present.

# CHAPTER EIGHT

# *Thank God for Science*

*Science without religion is lame, religion without science is blind.*

—Albert Einstein

THANK GOD FOR SCIENCE, AND THANK GOD FOR RELIGION and the sincerity of humanity to feel our own wonder. The two must come together now in the obvious clarity that the observer and the observed are arising in the one awesome reality. Heaven (if there is such a thing) and Earth are also arising in the one reality. We're not arguing for or against science or religion. Both can be warped by prejudice, and so both require the new framework: that the source and seen are One. That God and Sex are the same, meaning God and all tangible conditions are the same. We kind of know this—it's why we place flowers, the Sex of plants, on religious altars and give them to people we love. But we're not living it in our social arrangements or explicit understanding.

Science is a neutral tool that is being used by those who seek to dominate and control the earth and its peoples, rather than in service to a culture living in harmony with each other and our Mother Earth. To enjoy an authentic life, science doesn't have to go, religion doesn't have to go, your mind doesn't have to go, and Sex and relationship don't have to go. Up until now, there has been no other framework to see God, Sex, and Science. We have been like fishes in water, unable to describe the social thought structures that surround us. The fishes ask, "Oh what can water be"? And humans now must ask, "What is our reality?"

We've tracked how the scientific approach of observation and rationality was co-opted by commercial forces to serve their project of domination over nature, but even in the most benign articulations of science there is still the problem of the separation of the observer and the observed. As we said, this is useful when gathering data but not as a way to live. Imagine you're in an intimate sexual situation with someone who you like, love, and lust and who feels the same way about you. Now, imagine the other person has a checklist of 'techniques of intimacy' and begins working through them with you, commenting on your skills and writing notes in a small journal, perhaps sketching diagrams or taking close-up photos. It would obviously undermine the flow of intimate feeling between two people. This is what the scientific framework has done to our relationship with ourselves and the world. We are designed to feel intimate connection with everything, to feel ourselves merging in relatedness with everything, and to use our highly advanced nervous systems to feel all that there is to feel. Not to merely observe, analyze, or describe the world.

We can now have the best of both worlds: all the wonderful observations made by great life observers, and the ability to step away from the microscope and simply be in participatory relationship with it all. When we enjoy the wonderful scientist Sir David Attenborough and the clear besotted love he communicates for his subjects, we get the mood of the new scientist and the new science. We understand that science is for relationship and repair of Mother Nature's ecologies, participation *only* in the wonder of the universe. If I were to meet Sir David, I would say, "David, thank you for your new approach to science—for showing us an example." And I would tell him, "I am looking at you with the same passion and appreciation as you look at the butterflies, and I hope you see yourself in the same light."

I mean really, look at your hand. How and why does it exist? What is it? Why is it holding together like that? How does it know what to do in order to be a hand? How does it know how to regenerate and heal itself? Consider its intrinsic relationships as part of the whole body. Whatever it is, it functions beautifully, whether or not we understand it. The more we know, the more the mystery of the hand deepens (or the mystery of any other part of nature). We don't need to answer these questions so much as appreciate the effortless living quality that is prior to any description. We realize the essential unknowability of everything.

We need this sense of mystery in our life, and any doctrinal system that tries to eliminate it will be ultimately unsatisfying to its adherents. Religious people—creationists, for example—can hardly be blamed for wanting to hold onto a sense of wonder and mystery about the world, even as they ascribe this wonder to an absent Creator. Their anti-scientific religious fervor is merely a reaction to scientific modernity. Modernity's mechanistic reduction of the world and the body to mere physical matter and the elevation of the human mind to the only intelligent, morally valuable entity on Earth is unappealing. It has created the creationist reaction—and the irrationalities of the new-age reaction, even. No one wants to feel like they're an accidental meat sack in a mechanical universe. We intuit there is more to life than that. But without tangible feeling participation in the actual living, eternal quality of real conditions, we are just left making up more distracting abstract ideas to overlay onto the already-perfectly-good world. The dominance of the rational mindset creates deeply irrational subcultures.

So we are stuck oscillating between God and Sex, not suspecting that the two might be one. God without Sex is a meaningless and disempowering abstraction; Sex without God implies a vulgar and boring materialistic universe. And all the while the two are one. We could even say that perspectives dividing the two are *unscientific*, as true science is all about devotional investigation of the vast mysteries of the universe. The great physicist Albert Einstein, for example, was undoubtedly a mystic. The culture of modernity is a materialism that does not actually engage with the material, a materialism that cannot feel the full force of the world and has not noticed that, as William Blake wrote, "Everything that lives is Holy!" In contrast, the new science looks deeply into nature and finds indescribable beauty, logic, harmony, mystery, delight, and profundity.

## The Religion of Atheism

Because of its dark history and frequent denial of science, more and more young people around the world don't want to be associated with religion. Scorn for fundamentalisms and the rote religious gestures of older generations has put many younger people off their religious heritage entirely, and may cause them to identify as atheists. Disillusioned with religious power structures and hypocrisy, they resign themselves to the blandness of modern life, not recognizing how this too has been shaped by religious doctrine. We don't need to believe in any parental deity figures, but we do all need to connect our minds with their source (life) in some way. Without a means of actively addressing the cultural ideas we have inherited that tell us that the sublime is separate from the tangible, we will suffer the feeling of separation, as if looking on at life from the other end of the microscope. If we are willing to feel, we notice there is a sensation as if something is missing in our lives. Throwing out the separate God idea is not enough to live a sane and connected life. At its extreme, militant atheism promotes a joyless world. Even the human gene is only acting in self-interest now, apparently. A sense of nihilism, separation, and competition with others is naturalized, hiding the fact that this is a cultural perversion. The modern epidemic of apathy is a normal response when all that seems to be available is God without Sex (meaningless) or Sex without God (painful and deadening). For many, it is embarrassing to even admit these feelings, as we are supposed to be living the modern utopian dream.

Furthermore, prominent atheists can be very aggressive framing those who still believe in 'the God delusion' as stupid and naïve. People feel bullied by atheists as they do by any other religious orientation. Atheism is a belief system, one that hides behind the normalization of hyper-rationality in modern culture. The exclusionary concept of reason takes the place of God, and the atheist prides themselves on being the most reasonable person. But it's not reasonable to be grumpy and scornful of all those who don't agree with you, and portray them as 'deluded.' As another aggressive belief system, atheism is a religion and deserves all the criticism that religion deserves. The smugness of not believing in God as 'other' and the identity around that only springs from the need to be somebody, which only springs from the prior religious programming that you're not somebody. So the entire reactivity and solid anger of atheist activists like Richard Dawkins is itself an expression of their unaddressed religious conditioning. Atheists and religious fundamentalists alike need to come back to earth out of abstractions and embrace the sacredness that is all tangible conditions. When atheists truly don't believe in the God idea, they will stop reacting to it in adolescent anger.

## The New Science

In response to the denial of science, some people take up the position of the defense of science—but they're still unhappy. Science should be something we pick up and use when we want a certain way of understanding something. Instead it is our constant perspective, like a pair of glasses that we've forgotten we're wearing. We engage with everything as a detached observer, gathering data through our senses rather than experiencing intimacy, and not realizing that this is a specific cultural lens. Because everyone is doing it, and because everyone is suffering, it seems normal. But we are not meant to stay in detached observer mode. Once the data is collected, we step back and use it in life itself. Life is not for gathering data. It is for living. So stop looking! Start living.

Scientists have done such good work and are under assault from many angles from those who choose to ignore the facts (of climate change, for example). Science is under attack from both the anachronism of religious abstractions, and also the priests of money and progress. The two remain in collusion. We are fighting a losing battle. Consider the indignity of hundreds of millions flowing to the rebuilding of Notre Dame rather than into the rebuilding of the ecology and the economy to look after the needs of all. What is economy? It is to look after the needs of all the population and the needs of ecology. We need a new economics and a new ecology that provides for the needs of all people and the protection and restoration of Mother Nature's ecologies—serving the relationships that sustain us. We always have some kind of economy, so it needs to be one that serves nature and all her offspring, not just a few humans at the expense of nature and all others, imperiling the planet as a whole for the insane goals of short-term gain for a few. And not even really serving those few, because they remain dissatisfied and hungry for more. Humans cannot tolerate living within these thought structures. We cannot tolerate a sense of isolation from the land, from ourselves, from others, from the cosmos—from our species-being, no less. We are ready for the new science.

Putting science in its place as a tool, not a worldview, will do much to restore public faith in science when appropriate. For most of the twentieth century, the scientist was a kind of demi-god who could do no wrong. There was a time, not so long ago, when it was, "all hands on deck, we're heading into a bright future, and the scientists are leading the way!" Only after seeing hideous mass crimes against humanity amplified by technology did we begin to realize that science was not the savior we were looking for. We have seen the craters of atomic bombs and open-cast mines scarring the earth and have realized that the scientists are not in charge. The movement known as post-modernism pointed out that scientists were still people (often aged white men) with all their biases and prejudices. The illusion of objectivity was broken. We became aware that even when dealing in facts, human subjectivity is still involved in choosing which facts to look at and how to interpret them. In the belief that God was absent, science had been elevated into a new religion beyond its function, with all the blind enthusiasm once directed solely into religion. And so of course science is facing the same disillusionment that religion has faced, and the same dangerous desire to throw the baby out with the bathwater—politicians, for example, who encourage the public to treat science as an opinion factory when they want to justify continuing to burn coal (or any other profitable activity). From children believing everything our parents told us, we mature to adolescents believing nothing, and can now become adults, responsible for our own lives and not organized around any kind of parental authority.

Knowing we are adults and that no one is coming to save us, whether with a long white beard or a long white coat, we will be able to take responsibility for our actions in the world. We will make true progress on environmental issues, for example, when we stop expecting science to save us from them. I was struck to read the words of leading environmental scientist James Gustave Speth as he describes his own 'loss of faith':

> I used to think the top environmental problems were biodiversity loss, ecosystem collapse and climate change. I thought that with 30 years of good science we could address these problems. But I was wrong. The top environmental problems are selfishness, greed, and apathy... and to deal with those we need a spiritual and cultural transformation—and we scientists don't know how to do that.

In other words, we can only make use of the insights of science when we address the dissociation from and devaluation of the tangible that makes us feel we are isolated units, each one in it for themselves.

Hierarchy, both religious and scientific, has claimed authority and hoodwinked the people. But we live now in a time of 'post-post-modernism,' the Age of Relationship, where each person can directly experience their own reality, reality as it is, and will no longer need to put the priests of science or religion on a pedestal. Freed from these childish authority systems and the adolescent reaction to them, we are able to engage science and religion when we need them without any authority issues.

Even though I am critical of the old religious division of God and Sex that lives on in modern scientific ideologies, this is not to advocate for a return to a pre-scientific past or a rejection of reason and rationality as beautiful, useful functions of the mind. It is an argument to rid the world of mystification, including the scientific mystification that humans are the most valuable and purposeful beings, separate in kind from nature. For science to be of service to Mother Nature and all her species, it must be unhooked from the archaic assumptions that God or the divine is not here in the world, that the mind is separate from the body, and that our bodies and natural desires must be mastered. The body is an extreme intelligence. Nature is an unfathomable creative process. Left alone, the body does not want to learn or become anything. It is the power of the cosmos arising as a supreme intelligence that is always already in harmony with everything and everyone else. The human mind is obviously a beautiful function of nature and the body, not as its tyrannical ruler. Religious and scientific camps alike ignore the intrinsic intelligence and wonder of life, and so rather than oscillating between the two camps, we embrace the new science, which illuminates its own unknowable edges, creating more, not less mystery. The mystery is here, in your flesh and bones, in the natural cycles of embodied existence. We have the tools in our hands to redeem the suffering of the past and make a practical intervention in the world today.

You can be a scientist and look deeper and deeper into Mother Nature and the cosmos, and the more you look, the more you will be awestruck by the profundity, the power, the intelligence, and the indefinable beauty and harmony that is your own condition. You will have no choice but to give over to your own wonder.

# CHAPTER NINE

## *Back to the Garden*

*You have been forced to enter empty time.*
*The desire that drove you has relinquished.*
*There is nothing else to do now but rest*
*And patiently learn to receive the self*
*You have forsaken in the race of days.*
—John O'Donohue, 'For One Who is Exhausted, A Blessing'

One morning, my friend Lynn woke up and said to herself, "Wow, what if I didn't have to work on myself today." She lay there quietly in the morning light, without the usual thought structures of what she should do in order to be an okay or improved person. Suddenly, a great bolt of feeling energy moved through her, and she lay there basking in the livingness and intelligence of the whole body. She got up and went about her day simply in relationship to everyone and everything. That day, she was laughing at herself thinking about how much money she would save on workshops and beauty products. To this day, when her mind wanders into the patterns of future self-improvement, she can recognize it with some humor and go about her life free of these restraints. Life explodes through you from the inside once you recognize there is nothing to be liberated from and stop trying to improve yourself with all manner of sophisticated and gross seeking.

Modern culture inherited the religious distinction between God and Sex, so it is no surprise that we find ourselves menaced by a contemporary version of the Chain of Being. The new religion of self-help and trying to be perfect is unfortunately just the same as the religious search for God-realization or enlightenment, the invisible hierarchy of mind over matter. The assumption is that we are not there yet, that we are kicked out of Eden and wandering in the wilderness, and God is on our trail. We've been bad, and someone is watching and judging. Who is it? It seems like we have to work really, really hard in the social obsession with improvement to somehow redeem ourselves. The divine hierarchy has been repackaged in the form of unattainable ideals—the perfect body, the perfect mind, the perfect Sex, the perfect awareness, the perfect eyebrow, and the perfect iPhone. Our diligent commitment to working on ourselves is based on the same old patriarchal attempt to master our physicality. Whether the false promises are future God-realization or enlightenment, or just the trappings of the regular lifestyle, we ignore our given reality for a future that never arrives. The religious project disguised itself with a newfound claim to rationality—yet it remains completely unoriginal, repurposed within the secular paradigm as freedom from limits and domination of the body and nature.

The mind that you inherited from your social environment is busy with all kinds of speculations about life and how to find yourself. To be yourself is very easy; you don't have to do a thing. No effort is necessary, and you don't have to exercise your will. But try to be something other than what you are, and you have to do many unnecessary things and struggle a lot. To be yourself requires extraordinary intelligence. You are blessed with that intelligence; nobody need give it to you, and nobody can take it away from you.

All through secular culture, however, we find the inherited assumption that the body is unintelligent and uncreative, a dumb object or blunt instrument that the mind is entitled to use and abuse in pursuit of socially contrived goals. This culture of disregard for the body—or even hatred of the body, known as body dysmorphic disorder—expresses itself in the twin poles of self-improvement and transcendence—the desire to manipulate, improve upon, conquer, or escape the beautiful chaos of reality. We are yet to recognize the full sublimity and wonder of the body in all its relatedness—including Sex—and instead propose all sorts of arbitrary, unoriginal projects of mastery as the ultimate goal of human life. This search has made us miserable, which is then felt as a personal failure, rather than the logical outcome of constantly trying to be something that you are not.

So a vast invisible hierarchy persists, within which we hope to make progress according to arbitrary criteria. Happier, healthier, wealthier, sexier, more reasonable, more conscious, more qualified, more attractive—this is the new Chain of Being. Whenever we meet someone, we are working out where we fit against them in the imagined hierarchy, using comparisons with other people to feel good or bad about ourselves. Observe this happening in your own mind when you meet someone. Know that the hierarchy is socially contrived and you are both just the power of the cosmos happening. In the Buddhist/Vedantic perspective of 'no object, no subject to the object, reality only,' great truth has been spoken. As it says in the ancient Indian texts, the *Upanishads*, "Wherever there is an other, fear arises." There is really no other, there is just one life. God is not other. God is here as your Sex and your breath, and these are full and sufficient. Our practices of intimacy relieve us of the fear of others. Now, our forms come together in apparent individuation in the one reality. What a joy.

As infants, we absorb the social assumptions, patterns, and behaviors of our society. Everyone is feeling separate and living as if they are separate. It goes into us automatically and there is nothing we can do about it. Except for the blessed children of modern-day saints and sages, who are here and there, living in collaboration with each other. But for most, the sense of separation is painful. It is abusive to the living organism. Whether we are religious or not, we suffer this sense that something is missing in our lives, but we're not sure what. Because we feel separate, like something is not quite right, we are convinced that there is something to be worked on, something special that we have to do or some particular way to relate. So we start looking for it. We start exploring the religious method, the yogic method, the psychological method—or the regular methods of money, career, art, commerce, travel, higher education, food, sport, therapies, mindfulness, adventure, image maintenance, Sex, etc. But the search is the active denial of what is already the case. We long to relax into our own skins and live in the garden. We're still in Eden, but we've trashed it in our busy search. You get back to the garden by seeing that we are actually in the garden! I know this might seem implausible to those living in grey apartment blocks, but every body and every where is Mother Nature. And we will make harmonious living arrangements when we stop believing otherwise.

This is not to deny or judge any of our passions and activities, but if they are looking for a future attainment or happiness driven by an imaginary, socially implanted sense of separation, they become neurotic and only make matters worse. It's wonderful to wish to improve in our life disciplines, but we do not measure ourselves in their success or failure, because we are all already God's children in the garden. Link your life's work to this prior understanding, and you'll be good. I know you feel you'll be a hopeless slob if you don't drive yourself to achieve and improve, but it isn't true. It's the fear that haunts us and stops us resting, sleeping, and enjoying our relationships. In fact, when you stop measuring your happiness in the psychologies of future attainment, you will find that all skills dramatically increase. Your urgent passion to change the world and express your unique talents will be even more effective. Unhappiness is trying to be something you are not, and an approach to life that is constantly searching for the Holy Grail makes us rigid and easily knocked over, and then we give up. Discipline becomes easier freed from the psychology of success or failure as a person. Once we reject the false hierarchies, we are free to embrace our unique directions that may not be so socially valued. Only then is it possible to devote ourselves to our directions of choice with clarity, continuity, and lightness. But instead, we tend to get *seriously* busy trying to change ourselves to an arbitrary ideal that is not our own: return to nature, go within, be happy all the time, be eternally fulfilled, be the witness only, conquer the world, look like a sixteen year old, become a billionaire, or whatever else has been socially prescribed. The battle for approval rages on. These projects only obstruct relationship and Sex, because the starting premise of separation is not true and never was true. We are already the power of life happening, and so all projects towards future perfection are only running on the spot—mental busyness replicating the thought structures that prevent us from noticing the sublimity that is our condition. And those of us who have worked hard all of our lives toward a future wonderful result, well and good. This is the position of many creatives and hardworking people in our world. We've planted many fields with stooped backs. Now it is time to reap the harvest. Reap the harvest of your life. It is time.

## CHAPTER TEN

# *Death is Not the Enemy*

*In fear of death, man attempts to create eternity and glory for himself through religious institution, property, abuse of Mother Earth, and control of women. He does not come to peace with bodily existence or participate peacefully in the mystery power of the body or its passing. He therefore does not surrender to Earth and the great powers of Earth, the sublime regenerative force that is one hundred percent given and constant.*

—Mark Whitwell, The Promise

EVERYONE WHO HAS EVER LIVED HAS DIED, AND EVERYONE WHO is now living is going to die. This is not a design flaw! The cognition of this fact will move you to embrace reality as it is and not delay living your life. The usual life is organized around preventing death and not feeling the implications of death, which is that life is precious and immeasurable. "Do you need a little darkness to get you going?" wrote Mary Oliver. Death is there to push you to claim your life and embrace your life. The mind cannot control this life, the wildness and unpredictability that is upon us. We can only participate in it and enjoy the mysteries of life and death. Participation in this life prepares us for gracious death.

The engrained patriarchal patterning has tried to suppress, own, control, or ignore the feminine for centuries. Man flees from intimacy—whether through competitive career ambition, extreme gym workouts, warfare, absurd conquest missions like the desire to summit Mt Everest, the desire to leave a legacy of glory, all the way to space travel and the male obsession with sending tall buildings into the sky and (phallic) objects into outer space. Or the attempt to send his consciousness into space through spiritual seeking of alternate states. Man needs to give up the patriarchal quest to penetrate reality and learn to receive it instead. Only then he will truly penetrate/understand reality. Learning to receive will create your true legacy for humanity. No one cares what you put into orbit, but we do care how tenderly you can touch the earth. And because the patriarchal method has been promoted as the ideal, women too defend these roles of domination and control, whether for themselves or for men, and also need to surrender to the primacy of intimacy with the feminine.

The attempt to transcend and conquer the messy world of our lives is born out of the fear of death. Fear of death is what creates secular culture's negative relationship to aging and bodily decline and keeps us busy trying to avoid them in the cult of youth. Fear of death lurks beneath the feeling that there is something negative about growing old, an insane proposition when aging is the most natural process of life, and a sign of success in that we have survived! We pretend aging is not happening, while secretly fighting it with all we've got. But we are actually not in charge here; aging cannot be controlled, and so within the modern obsession with control over nature, it is associated with a sense of failure. Death too, although I suppose we are no longer around to feel bad about that one. But everyone else does, and sometimes those who die are even resented for having 'failed' to beat death. Modern-day beauty standards encourage us to 'fight the seven signs of aging,' and cultures around the world have forced bodies into ridiculous contortions in the attempt to thwart the natural passage of time. These thought structures have gone into us whether we are male or female, but are often particularly felt by women, as they have been led to associate so much self-worth with physical appearance and youthfulness. As the American writer Joan Didion comments in her memoir, *Blue Nights*:

> Aging and its evidence remain life's most predictable events, yet they also remain matters we prefer to leave unmentioned, unexplored: I have watched tears flood the eyes of grown women, loved women, women of talent and accomplishment, for no reason other than that a small child in the room, more often than not an adored niece or nephew, has just described them as 'wrinkly,' or asked how old they are. When we are asked this question we are always undone by its innocence, somehow shamed by the clear bell-like tones in which it is asked. What shames us is this: the answer we give is never innocent. The answer we give is unclear, evasive, even guilty.

Consider the very different approach we take when looking at other forms of life, such as trees. We look at a slim young sapling and admire its freshness and beauty; we look at a tall tree in the prime of forest life and admire its strength and beauty; and we look at a great elder tree and admire its incredible complexity, wisdom, and radiance as a living form. We look at a tree near the end of its natural life and marvel at the fact it is there at all, grateful to have a moment in its profound company. There is no sense of feeling like it 'should' look anything like the sapling. However, because we have sought to locate the sacred somewhere outside of the facts of human birth and death, the same rich lifecycle is not recognized when it comes to human beings.

In some indigenous cultures, like the Māori culture of my home country of Aotearoa (New Zealand), those over the age of sixty are venerated as *Kaumātua*—as elders who carry the wisdom of their life and the language, *tikanga* (correct customs) and tradition of the community. They are accorded a social role of leadership and *mana* (dignity) in their community and *whānau* (extended family).

***

We can clearly see the mass denial of aging and death in the projects of technological transcendence being hatched in Silicon Valley between tech oligarchs and the world's best scientific minds. Scientists are enrolled in projects of life-extension, life-enhancement, anti-aging technologies, and even projects of total transcendence of the body and death. Some crazy people plan to overcome death completely—the most extreme gesture of life denial. The denial and suppression of aging and death arises from the mind's acculturated sense that it is a separate, superior faculty attached to an imperfect, unintelligent, decaying vessel. But life is the nurturing, and everything about life is nurturing, including pain, which keeps us safe and is the healing process. Illness is also the process of healing. The body is throwing out what it doesn't need. And if illness resolves into death, then death is the ultimate nurturing event of our life. It is being held in the arms of Mother, who takes us home. Death is a human need that gives profound dignity to the life we have lived. To want more quantity of life betrays a lack of quality of life. To see the human condition as a set of limitations and problems to be solved is a patently ridiculous mistake. To see limitations where there is in fact beauty, wonder, creativity, and unfathomable intelligence; to see separation where there is whole body/mind unity; to see separation where eternity is arising in the present moment as the present body: these indicate a profound error. Developments in the field of technological manipulation and control are an indication of confusion, not progress. There is nothing wrong with technology, but it is being developed and wielded by a culture committed to abusing its own living flesh. If we would turn their scientific enquiry to utter intimacy with our own reality and the polarity of all opposites, we would be back in the garden and able to live in peace in this abundant paradise. If the scientists and technologists would utilize their disciplines to spread and distribute this understanding to the whole of humanity, then we'd all get home.

CHAPTER ELEVEN

# *Pain is Not the Enemy*

*If you evade suffering you also evade the chance of joy. Pleasure you may get, or pleasures, but you will not be fulfilled. You will not know what it is to come home.*

—Ursula Le Guin, The Dispossessed

WE DO NOT GET TO CHOOSE OUR EMOTIONS. THEY ARE PART OF nature's intelligence and valid responses to the events of our lives. In modern life, we are taught to try to avoid pain and that a life free from pain and difficult emotions is the goal. But the search for a painless life only inflicts pain upon the body and obstructs its nurturing, self-healing, intrinsic intelligence. Trying to sedate wild creatures just makes them angry. New-age ideologies, like the cult of positive thinking, suggest that you have caused your suffering through negative thoughts or bad karmas and are wrong to have honest emotions like fear, anger, pain, and grief. These cults make us ashamed of our pain and repress it. But there is no way around pain except through it. It's like the Bear Hunt: "We've got to go through it." We must surrender to the conditions of real emotion, whatever they are.

In avoidance of our real pain, we inflict more pain on ourselves. The idea that mind is the source of intelligence and worth reduces the physical body to an instrument, something that we reside in, or own.

Something that must be engineered to some higher purpose as if it is lower. We hope that we can tell our bodies what they ought to feel, avoiding our real pain. From here we take up all kinds of hobbies to bully the body to try and make it conform to our inherited agendas. Everywhere we look, we are bombarded with messages encouraging us to push beyond our natural limits. At the mild end of the spectrum this looks like the refusal to listen to the body's needs and desires—the desire for rest, sleep, intimacy, nourishment, Sex, a break from work—even a toilet break. Some examples: the yoga teacher telling students to 'find their edge' and then go beyond it; the young woman going to the gym every day after work despite feeling exhausted; the man adopting strict dietary regimes in pursuit of perfect health and the maintenance of peak performance; or the many varieties of eating disorder that punish and control the body. At the extreme end is the refusal to accept and go through the natural human processes of emotions, the fire of relationship, and the challenges of illness, aging, and death. It takes archetypal form as the mad scientist attempting to go beyond nature's limits, first characterized by Mary Shelley in Dr. Frankenstein and his Creature. The uncontrollable, undeniably sexual world of our animal bodies is an embarrassment to the dream of mastery—the search for a state of future perfection that once carried the label 'heaven' or enlightenment.

Through understanding and feeling that the fullness and wonder of life is already manifesting in us, as us, we are able to relinquish the model that sees the body as a blunt instrument. It is no longer relevant. We can relax from the myriad projects of manipulation and self-improvement—whether through exaggerated exercise, speed reading, compulsive online course consumption, dieting, surgery—and let the vast beauty, intelligence and relatedness of the body flourish. Even the function of learning has been corrupted as a means of progress up the Chain of Being. We think that the body has to learn something, realize something, or adapt to something clever, as if the body is not already a vast intelligence. The body doesn't want be taught anything, and the body doesn't need to know anything. The sense that it needs to is implanted by the belief that it is lower. When we stop trying to teach or liberate the body, extraordinary power is available to us and explodes through our body and mind.

So much stress is caused by the mind's imagined sense that it is attached to an imperfect or unintelligent body. Even saying we must love our 'flaws' is still defining ourselves in relation to someone else's ideals. Who said they were flaws! Give Mother Nature a break. She is as she is, and the first act of ecology occurs in relation to receiving our own form. These bodies are the wild of Mother Nature. Consider how the whole body is already in harmony with the rest of existence—the green world, the sun, the air, food, light, water and any unseen or intangible aspects of the cosmos. Or how the body knows exactly what to do with sunlight. We do not have to establish our relationship with the sun. It is simply given. We are built and sustained by light; literal light is received by all our cells. On every inhale we receive the light. On every exhale we give to the light. We are at one with the sun. The source. In every moment, your body is in a profound relationship with light and with air. Air is kissing your lungs and your blood. Your body knows what to do with air, without any conscious intervention. This is the natural state. It is your condition, no matter what the mind is up to. So we don't need any more ideologies of self-improvement. The unoriginal idea that the supreme goal of human life is the transcendence of nature's honest movements actually inhibits our capacity to feel. We need intimacy and receptivity, that's all.

***

When you look at how we deal with emotions, it is obvious that 'mind over matter' is not working for us, but rather causing mental illness and unhappiness. The belief that control over the emotions is even possible has left millions of justifiably unhappy people feeling guilty for their pain, rather than acting on it. As J. Krishnamurti said, "It is no measure of health to be well adjusted to a profoundly sick society." If our minds are always geared towards future states of bliss and socially contrived ideals, then we will deny the experiences that life is presenting. There is only one switch for feeling, on or off! What you feel is what you feel, and everything is the truth. Our capacity for feeling is infinite, and so it is only through engaging in the full spectrum of feeling that we can feel the infinite. Emotions and feelings, even if they are extremely uncomfortable, are absolutely valid and necessary in life. They are natural. They are nature's way of protecting you. Fear is the way the organism protects itself. Anger is a valid function to protect ourselves and others from abuse. Pain is nature's way of healing; it is literal biochemical processes taking place in our biology. Without pain, we wouldn't know to take our hand out of the fire. We wouldn't know that society is sick. Pain demands its own reduction. Thank God for our pain, because it leads us to practice intimate connection, the lack of which causes the pain. It leads us to create intelligent change. If we spend a lifetime avoiding pain, we become ill-equipped to cope with grief, to feel joy or sublime communion, or to feel anything much at all. Pain is not the enemy. We can co-operate with and honor pain, knowing that the goal of nature is regeneration and health. Peace and fulfilment come from accepting the pain that is part of the human lifecycle. When we accept the fact of our situation, we can meet the intensity of life, knowing that we are supported by a great nurturing force. Here we find that acceptance and surrender to nature in fact makes us stronger. We are in good hands in this universe.

In modern life's obsession with avoiding pain, we have become habituated to particular emotions and their addictive biochemistries, in the same way as any other addiction. We usually do not move through the natural sequence of emotion; instead we get stuck. The natural sequence of emotional response to difficult circumstances is usually this: numbness, fear, anger, pain, grief, compassion, forgiveness, and love. We must move through this natural sequence without getting stuck in any one particular emotion. At each stage we can predict the next fundamental emotion or the cause of the emotion we are presently in. The point is to fully participate in whichever emotional condition we are in, whilst recognizing that it is a process to be moved through gracefully. I say 'get to grief' as quickly as possible. Grief for the whole shoddy deal dished up to all of humanity. In grief, the gifts of compassion arise for yourself and everybody. This is not to say that we can bypass the other emotions—it is a process, not a hierarchy. Every stage is valid and true. We have to get to grief through the honest sequence, no matter how difficult these feelings are.

Often when we are in pain, we look to spiritual teachers to help us. But when there is a hierarchical teaching dynamic, neither teacher nor student are able to go through the honest sequence of emotions. The teacher will be stuck trying to maintain an ideal image so as not to fall off the pedestal. The student will be stuck trying to perform whatever they think will gain the approval of the teacher, as we learned to do to try and keep our parents happy. Neither is able to be real, and so life's natural process of resolution and release is obstructed.

Neither 'spiritual' practices of detachment nor secular practices of mastery equip us with the sensitivities required to meet difficult emotions. In fact, by encouraging us to rise above the body or look towards idealized future states of endless bliss or perpetual glossy magazine happiness, they only make matters worse. When we do feel terribly angry or unhappy or depressed, we are often made to feel worse, as if we should always be smiling like the Buddha. Many spiritual teachers tell us that our emotions are not real or that they are a symptom of our failure to identify with our 'true self.' And modern culture often medicalizes our emotions without acknowledging their underlying cause—grief, for example, is a profound and normal process to go through when a loved one dies, that needs time to be felt, rather than to be pathologized or medicated. We need this space for grief in the face of death, but it is also appropriate to feel grief just in the observation of the dreadful suffering in our world. If we allow grief, compassion can arise naturally. Conventional medicine and conventional religion prescribe the opium for the masses, 'helping' them avoid feeling by any means possible. They do not give us the means to acknowledge the emotional difficulties of our lives, nor the tools to move towards grief, compassion, and love. Our culture instead provides a glut of options to move us back in the other direction, toward numbness.

What we need is a practice of immersion in all tangible conditions, including our real and necessary emotions. This kind of intimacy with ourselves and others is what allows for emotional digestion. We develop the required strength at the same time as the required receptivity that together are needed in order to experience this life. If we are willing to feel them, our emotions take us to love, the absolute condition, the one reality in which everything is happening, including pain. By the gentleness of daily discipline, we can learn to participate in the natural intimacies that have already been given. The resulting intimacy with your breath and body develops an intimacy with yourself. The practice may raise difficult emotions in us that we have been holding in, unable to digest up until this point. Yet this intimate connection is the great healing. It is like when we are struggling and finally burst into tears when someone is kind to us—but with ourselves. The result is regeneration and health, the nature of nature.

CHAPTER TWELVE

# *The World Cult of Meditation*

*I know, you never intended to be in this world.*
*But you're in it all the same.*

*So why not get started immediately.*

*I mean, belonging to it.*
*There is so much to admire, to weep over.*

*And to write music or poems about.*

*Bless the feet that take you to and fro*
*Bless the eyes and the listening ears.*
*Bless the tongue, the marvel of taste.*
*Bless touching.*

*You could live a hundred years, it's happened.*
*Or not.*
*I am speaking from the fortunate platform of many years,*
*none of which, I think, I ever wasted.*
*Do you need a prod?*
*Do you need a little darkness to get you going?*
*Let me be as urgent as a knife, then, and remind you of Keats,*
*so single of purpose and thinking, for a while,*
*he had a lifetime.*

—Mary Oliver, 'The Fourth Sign of the Zodiac' (Part 3)

THE POINT OF LIFE IS TO EMBRACE EXPERIENCE, NOT TO DETACH from it. It is intimacy we need, not meditation. Intimacy, not philosophy. Intimacy, not mindfulness. Intimacy, not positive thinking. In intimacy, all of these gifts arise. The world cults of meditation and mindfulness have put humanity in conflict with our own reality. Recall that even the most modern iterations of meditation and mindfulness still come from a legacy of womanless men living dissociated lives away from society. Instead of embracing our lives, these cultures have promoted only the 'witnessing' of experience, which inherently is a project of dissociation. The mere fact that you are witnessing your experience implies you are separate from it. Imagine going on a date with someone who remained merely 'aware' of you. It would be boring at best, psychopathic at worst. Or imagine if your intimate partner was only ever 'aware' of you—with commentary perhaps. (Unfortunately, we don't have to try very hard to imagine this, a sign of the world success of this philosophical project.) Swathed in spiritual superiority, the project of detachment distracts us from enjoying our inherent intimacy with life. It is these archaic doctrines of renunciation that the world religions are based on. The promise of Buddhist and Christian monastic life is that if you abide as the witness only to all arising conditions, then you will know awareness itself, consciousness itself, God, the absolute, what-have-you.

The reason meditation cults have found such a ready audience in secular society is because they confirm the scientific/religious mind's sense of detachment from nature and experience, and then gild this imaginary separation with the glamour of both neuroscientific research and the aggression of self-improvement-based Buddhism (the attainment of higher states). And, of course, because people are in pain and looking for a way out of it. Like selling alcohol, it exploits the suffering and gullibility of the people. It must be acknowledged that the merchandizing of inner peace has started yet another war raging within and without. Advertisements for mindfulness training present young, smiling, beatific, sexy women sitting in a cornfield, atop a mountain, or on a clean white background—yet another ideal to work towards or measure yourself against.

Elsewhere, the goals of the great wisdom teachings have been presented as impossible ideals for those of us leading 'normal' lives.

Shadowy concepts like enlightenment stand in stark contrast to the lives we are actually living. We hear that a world of spiritual joy awaits us—somewhere between the Buddha's knowing smile and the abundant lifestyles of a beautiful few who trained at the feet of mysterious masters—but meanwhile we are bound to the routines of working, studying, having relationships, raising children, and washing the dishes. 'Successful' meditators seem to have a luminosity and otherworldly detachment that we seek to emulate. But as we saw earlier, this apparent 'success' is usually concentrated in an inner knowing of existence that entails 'going within' at the expense of 'external' conditions. Fair enough, but we are discussing the full radiance of Life and how existence embraces *all* directions and *all* things tangible and intangible. Inner states of aloofness* and inner luminosity have been glamourized by a select few, leaving everyone else stuck in a lifetime of struggle with idealisms. But it is everyone's birthright to embrace the unfolding of Life in all directions. In intimacy with tangible conditions the inner light can be easily felt by ordinary people.

People discover that no matter how hard they try to be the unattached observer, to stand outside the stream of daily life, to 'observe their thoughts', the demands of domesticity require involvement in this material world. Dinner does not cook itself. Uninformed spiritual teachers have reduced everyday life—food, family, work, relationships, and Sex—to merely the content of your awareness training or, worse, as an obstruction to it. This is a mistake. These seemingly mundane activities *are* your reality, full and complete in themselves, not a means to an end or an obstruction on some imaginary path. The great advice from the wisdom traditions of humanity is to fully take on and merge with your experience, to embrace experience and get amongst it rather than merely to be mindful of it or witness only. "Why not get started immediately," writes our beloved Mary Oliver.

Mindfulness has become a very popular practice, one that can be useful in providing temporary relief from turbulent thoughts. And many of us first encounter spiritual practice through meditation to quiet the mind. It calms the system, and this is valid, just as a glass

---

* aloof *(adjective):* conspicuously uninvolved

of wine or a massage may be valid. But we need more than this. We need intimacy. We need to address the apparent lack of connection that caused all the turbulent thoughts in the first place. Chaotic and compulsive thinking is not a design flaw in the human system that we must medicate or meditate our distance from. It is the intelligence of the body-mind letting us know that our mind has become dissociated from its source, and needs to participate in what is actually going on. The mind is overactive because it thinks there is somewhere to get to and it is trying to help us get there. The solution is releasing all the engrained doctrines towards future sublimities and practicing participatory embrace of all, not tuning out of the whole mess for a fragile inner peace. When the children are fighting, we cannot just shut ourselves in our rooms and hope they figure it out. We need to get involved in bringing active peace to the situation by addressing the source of conflict. This is the situation in our minds.

Ultimately, the cost of the breathing room provided by meditative practice is the reinforcement of the dissociation that causes the pain in the first place. Consider the example of relationship. If you're in the usual sexual relationship of control, uncertainty, jealousy, conflict, casualness, neurotic clinging, 'you don't love me' showdowns, and even abuse, then the thought of being single will appeal. Being single promises relief from relationship dysfunction. But those are not the only two options! Sublime love relationship *is* possible. And the ambiguity created in relationship by one or the other person being tempted towards the 'peace' and 'space' of singledom *is* usually what creates all the relationship drama that we want to escape from. In the same way, the movement away from actual tangible conditions to escape all the drama *creates* the drama. People are leaving their spouses to go on heroic meditation retreats, hoping this will somehow give them the skills to step out of the inherited cycles of reactivity and numbness, not realizing that the temporary peace that may be achieved through a strange and extreme circumstance will make them only more reactive when they return to their partner, who will probably appear to be only more difficult in their feeling of abandonment and spiritual inferiority. Or we may attend endless yoga or meditation workshops in exotic locations, looking for the ability to relate to the very people we have left behind. So many relationships have been destroyed by one of the partners being seduced by enlightenment—the socially contrived desire to feel something else and be someone else rather than be with the beloved who is right in front of them. Who is the very form of God who is available for them. The search for God away from Sex has made Sex toxic, fueling the desire to escape it, in an endless dysfunctional cycle. And yet: peace is possible in intimacy. 'Immersion in chaos' versus 'detached observation of chaos' are not our only two options.

In truth, the content of our troubled minds is caused by a lack of intimacy and a desire for connection. Think about it. What troubles your mind? What fills your journal? We all seek ways to break down the barriers between us and we all want to be received by our friends and family as the wonder of life that we are. In turn, we all want to be able to give love to those around us. In intimacy, thinking becomes clear and useful and all things are given. When we feel loved and are able to love, we are at peace. When we feel separate, our minds go crazy. Intimacy cuts through your troubles like a hot knife through butter. It is the embrace that ends an argument abruptly and completely, not observation, analysis, or dissociation from an argument ('I am not the one arguing, I am consciousness itself').

Therefore, what we need is a philosophy of intimacy, not a philosophy of detachment. Clarity of mind arises through embracing our tangible connection to what is already right here. We prioritize our relationship to our own embodiment and our relationship with others, including and especially intimate sexual union. This may be a little hard to swallow for those of us who have experienced relief from total identification with our own chaotic thought patterns and who are familiar with the scientific research showing how mindfulness brings relief. There is nothing wrong with this relief. But there is so much more that is available to us! I am speaking to you as a friend with the utmost respect for sincerely held practices and all sincere people. I am asking you simply to unhook these practices from the limiting thought structures by which they have been co-opted and commodified. And which are now so widespread that they are branded into our psyche as what meditation IS. We can now turn the dissociative practices of transcendence and awareness in the opposite direction of connection to and caring for Mother Nature and life on Earth.

The earliest roots of most modern meditation techniques and teachings lie in the ancient Indian culture of Veda, a culture where God, deity, guru, spouse, the body, and the whole seen and unseen elemental world were seen to arise as One reality. Besotted relationship with all was the way of this culture, not contemplation toward a future result, where human life and all life is imagined to be less. Meditation is action, which may well turn into quiet times of *motiveless* sitting—self-abiding in and as the absolute condition that is arising as the whole body in its intrinsic harmony and connection with the whole of life. That is, self-abiding *in relationship.* It does not exist as a practice by itself, however. The power of mindfulness meditation arises naturally as part of one's overall life, a gift of our intimacy with our life.

Contemporary meditation culture has provided a fertile ground for ideas of inadequacy and self-improvement to flourish in. We must unqualify our practices of relationship from all doctrines of self-improvement or spiritual attainment. Beware of thoughts like 'I should be meditating,' 'I should be finding peace' or 'I'm terrible at meditating' or 'I need to be more present.' Or, conversely, 'I am a cool dude meditator now.' The efforts of meditation create the personality or identity of 'I am a meditator, trying to be spiritual'. Every time you sit down to meditate, you are reinforcing the chains of assumption that you are bound and not yet free. That you have to do something on yourself in order to get free one day in the future. When you do experience temporary successes—blisses or *samadhi*—those chains turn from iron chains to golden chains. You're enamored by the gold, and they're harder to get off. Be brave enough to throw it all out. Because God is not absent. You live in utter relatedness right now. Your body, left alone, is already perfectly receptive to experience. Union has already happened. What is meditation? It is the mind and body's intrinsic feeling-connection to what is already the case, the natural state. It cannot be willfully done, but arises naturally in a life of intimate connection. It is there in all natural intimacies, from a kiss, to the touch of a leaf, or the wind on your legs. Just as you cannot willfully put yourself to sleep, you cannot meditate. Trying to sleep will prevent sleep. Trying to meditate will prevent meditation. It arises naturally as a gift when the conditions of intimacy are present. When you link the breath to the whole body, the mind automatically follows the breath. The mind therefore gets linked to the whole body, which is the power, the intelligence, and the beauty and harmony of the cosmos. The mind feels itself to be arising as a function of its source, which is Life itself. There is no problem to mind. You don't need to keep reminding yourself to 'be here now.' You *are* here now.

So we can stop the endless observation and analysis of the social limits that you were born into and that now seem to affect you or even be your identity. We can stop the long conversations about them with others who feel affected. We can stop the tortured process of trying to be aware. This is the preoccupation now of society even in its spiritual old-world, new-age products and across the secular world of intelligent young people. We do not need to dissect and unpack all of our inherited neuroses—familial or social. We do not need to engage in long arguments with others to try and make them become more aware. Awareness alone of social thought structures and what is wrong with the world is not the point. We need the practical means to move in a different direction, to embrace the perfection of our lives.

Without the practice of besotted intimacy to distract us from our imagined limitations, we are stranded somewhere between self-hatred and irony. As the American writer David Foster Wallace once said, irony is "the song of a bird who enjoys being in the cage." Do not let the world's toxicity touch your heart, but participate and get involved in the wonder of the given reality and the life of your community. Embrace your life; do not step back from it or feel trapped within the thought structures and divisions put in you by the powers that be. If you do meditate, sit in a full feeling of the relationships you love, the person or people that you love and who love you, and/or all the beauty of the natural world that you also love and are dependent on. This way you are meditating in relationship with something, not just being aware of it. The practice of life is to merge with perception (body, breath, and relationship in that order). The mind is for this merging. It is not for dissociating.

I want to assure meditators and practitioners of mindfulness that your skill in meditation will deeply improve when the practices of intimacy with body, breath, and relationship are prioritized. Then the gifts of meditation arise spontaneously and easily. You will find yourself to be at one with reality itself, the natural state. Many meditators I know have been initially resistant to this idea, and it is even painful for them to consider that their practices may not be as fruitful as they hope. Those with decades of meditation experience and some sensitivity, however, inevitably come to feel as though they have hit a wall. Their meditation itself may be deep and enjoyable, but it doesn't seem to be transforming their life and existential experience in the way they hoped for. Something is not quite right. Such practitioners have been very ready to listen to this argument and experiment with a practice of intimacy. Physical practices have been taught with such vulgar patterning by gymnastic cults led by domineering men (and women). It comes as no surprise that people with sensitivity of meditative practice have felt valid distaste or felt physical practices to be irrelevant to them. The vulgarity of most practices on offer has only served to reinforce the meditator's belief that the body is lesser or 'gross,' and their need to retreat to the subtle self within—in much the same way as the vulgarities of sex performance and the burden of pornography has caused those with sensitivity to retreat into celibacy. Given the choice between God and Sex, the meditators have chosen God (or consciousness, or the void, or the absolute, or 'no-thingness,' or the witness only, or the divine). But the choice does not need to be made, and has itself stripped sacredness from the world and given license to use and abuse it. Man's search for heaven has created a hell of this abundant paradise. Understanding that God and Sex belong together, because they are together in reality, will heal both for everybody on Earth. The awareness that we are One with Mother Nature—that we *are* nature, not the witness of her—will come as a gift, enabling us to truly participate in her ecologies. This will save the human species and the many others currently victimized by the dissociative search for escape from 'worldly' conditions.

CHAPTER THIRTEEN

# *Merging with Experience*

*If the doors of perception were cleansed*
*every thing would appear to man as it is, Infinite.*

—William Blake, *The Marriage of Heaven and Hell*

*Nay I see that God is in all Creatures, Man and Beast,*
*Fish and Fowle, and every green thing, from the highest Cedar*
*to the Ivey on the wall; and that God is the life and being of them all,*
*and that God doth really dwell, and if you will personally...*
*in them all, and hath Being no where else out of the Creatures.*

—The 'Ranter' Jacob Bauthumley, England, 1650

WE HAVE ALL EXPERIENCED THOSE MOMENTS IN LIFE WHERE WE are completely immersed in what we are doing, when our whole attention—mind and body—is synchronistically given over to what is in front of us. For some of us, this happens when we hear beautiful music, when we create stories or paint, when we make love or spend time with our intimate partner, or when we are suddenly caught by the beauty of the sunset or absorbed in an impressive piece of architecture. When you move in a direction of your choice with continuity and merge with your experience, then distraction, fluctuations of mind, and the mental limitations that we have inherited from our social patterning fall away. When we are intimate with our experience, we feel like we know it directly; we experience life without mediating abstractions. Our ancient ancestors understood this to be one of the greatest pleasures in life and, in fact, the whole point of life! The reason is that when we merge with the object of our experience and feel like we know it at a deep level, the same depth of knowledge occurs at the level of the perceiver. By being intimate with our experience we become intimate with ourselves. We then come to know the knower of that experience: Life, Consciousness, God. Intimacy with the world reveals our true nature. God stops being an abstract concept or an 'other.' The experience and the experiencer are joined in the recognition that they are one.

Our ancient ancestors also understood that there must be a practical means for individuals to participate in this beautiful human capability. This is even more true in our modern times, where our attention and sense of connection to our experience feels increasingly lanced by the forces of advertisement, the addictive design of social media, and the pressures of work. Many of us feel distracted and hare-brained. We may find it hard to come into intimate relationship with anything other than our neurosis! But it's not our fault: the dualistic thought structures of secular and religious society have done a lot to diminish our attentiveness to the way the whole body feels, experiences, and knows our experience. Regardless, the desire to merge with our experience is within all of us. It is a powerful driving force and it must have its way. We don't want to spend our days feeling separate, like a spectator to our own lives. And if we don't have a practical way to participate in this exquisite human drive—our birthright, no less—then it will manifest in all sorts of aberrant and exaggerated ways.

The impulse to consume mind-altering drugs (which includes alcohol) often derives from the desire to focus in, move with continuity, and merge with our experience. Many mind-altering substances curb the discursive habits of our thinking, loosening the restrictive grip of the social mind on the whole body and allowing the entire feeling human organism to come into play. Similarly, those who partake in extreme adventure sports involving high levels of danger—whether it be high-speed mountain biking, base-jumping, motor-racing, river-rafting, climbing Mount Everest, and the like—often report a highly enjoyable and heightened sense of being at one with their experience. These sports create a situation in which the individual puts their body, if not their entire life, at extreme physical risk and so the whole body hones in on the experience out of necessity. The drive to do such things is simply to be able to feel the union with experience, in these cases exaggerated. It gives a sense of the one who is experiencing.

Exaggerated sexual activity can also produce fleeting peak experiences, creating addiction to pornographic performance. Just like throwing ourselves out of airplanes, it is unnecessary and dangerous and only done in order to feel that glimpse of reality. And because it is only a glimpse, it creates urgency and addiction to experience it again. Often the drastic activities we undertake to try and feel these moments of union frighten and numb our nervous systems, thereby becoming increasingly ineffective over time and leaving us looking for the next, more extreme way to feel something.

I want to assure you that you don't have to take mind-altering drugs or risk your life and limb in exaggerated experiences in order to get this feeling of yourself in harmony with everything. In fact, these peak experiences can make us more miserable by throwing mundane everyday life into glum contrast. Through practice of intimacy, we can feel our sense of harmonious merging with all in a sustainable and non-dramatic everyday way. Because we *are* merged. We are in harmony. So all we need is participation in the natural, already-given relationships and harmonies of our everyday life. Moving and breathing and relating to the natural world, including each other, is accessible to everyone, easily done, and requires no special skill or equipment. No parachutes or ambulances required.

When we rely on peak experiences to get a glimpse of the harmony that is there all the time, we become miserable, addicted, and dangerous to ourselves and others. We need to have an easy way to participate in our innate oneness with all without needing to try and get it, as if it is something temporary, artificial, manufactured, exaggerated, induced, or generally outside of the sphere of everyday life. To merge and be at one with our experience must be seen as normal, free, and easy. There is nothing wrong with adventure sports, for example, but we will be able to make safer and freer decisions around our participation in them when we are not depending on them to feel merged with Life. We already are Life, so there must be simpler ways.

Physical practices are essentially about free participation in the breath. To be with the breath is to be with that which is breathing us. The body remains soft and structured around the breath movement, while the moving anatomy serves the breath process. The body movement is the breath movement, and vice versa. The mind can then feel its own source and its own nature. Movement with breath may be some work but not a struggle. The breath is the gauge to the moving anatomy. The challenge is within the breath limits, not in the musculature. Practices are designed for the individual and tailored to be within anyone's capability. The practice is adapted to the individual, not the individual to the practice. It is not an attempt to impose the mind's predetermined structuring or any cultural proposition on the body. The breath, too, should not be overly controlled, but flow smoothly within comfortably managed breath ratios. The goal of these practices is to *unqualify* the organism of mind, not qualify it. This occurs through intimacy with body, breath, and mind as one process. Finally, this goal itself is seen to be an obstruction and unnecessary because the living organism already stands in its intelligence: the natural state. There are no steps to be taken.

These matters need to be learned in person from someone who cares about you, who is not imposing their own agenda or predefined patterns on you. Be aware that there are many well-meaning people who want to sell you prepackaged, stylized patterns and the experiences induced by them, in the same addictive model of extreme sport or drugs. The simplicity of merging with experience through movement and breath are not the duplication of anyone's stylized patterns or any social patterning at all. And the purpose is to learn to feel your life as it is, to become feeling in life. And even to feel all that there is to feel—infinity itself, arising as every thing. God and Sex are indeed one.

## CHAPTER FOURTEEN

# *The Heart's Embrace of Ordinary Conditions*

*My Deare One.*

*All or None.*

*Every one under the Sunne.*

*Mine own.*

—The 'Ranter' Abiezer Coppe, *A Fiery Flying Roll,* England, 1650

THE HEART IS THE FIRST CELL OF LIFE THAT APPEARED WHEN YOU appeared from the mystic perfect harmony of male-female, the nurturing power of life. It is known in the traditions as the 'heart on the right' (the *hridaya*), and is distinct from the physical heart muscle and the energy center known as the heart *chakra* in the midpoint of the chest. From this depth, the nurturing force of life was initiated and flows now in all directions to form the whole body, like a flower in full bloom. The heart is the origin of all opposites, the body's portal to all of the powers and mysteries of the cosmos that are arising as the whole body and all its relatedness. In death, the body drops and the source heart and its flow remains in its infinite condition.

For most of modern history, the heart has been overlooked as the high locus of religious and spiritual realization due to the predominant patriarchal view of life as a process of ascent through the body to the crown and beyond. The base of the body (reproductive organs, for example) is sought to be sublimated, as if lower is negative, a life-denying assumption. Either that, or patriarchal contemplative cultures (such as those inspired by Indian sage Ramana Maharshi [1879-1950]) have sought to gain realization through efforts of mind. The view of such cultures has been that by stepping back from experience and merely witnessing all arising conditions, the source or heart that Ramana spoke of can be realized, as if it is obscured by our tangible world. All this creates is a fragile kind of peace stemming from dissociation.

## The Heart's Response to Grace

I recently saw a YouTube video in which the actor Jim Carrey gets really excited about having discovered a spiritual teacher. It seems that in reading and listening to him, Carrey had felt a sudden "wake-up" moment. He realized that he was the power of the cosmos, consciousness itself. In that blissful moment, he felt a deep sense of peace and freedom from all his concerns. But in recounting the story, Carrey makes a parody of himself. He grits his teeth, makes a fierce face, and says, "I have been trying to get back there ever since." Ever the brilliant comic, Carrey cracked me up by expressing the very human dilemma we are in. We have our high moments of clear insight and wonderful inspiration from all kinds of influences. But then life as usual drones on in the troubled mind. And there our attention seems to fixate most. Sometimes inspirations can even make matters worse because we feel how mediocre daily life seems to be compared to our 'peak' experience.

Years ago in India, my teacher used to say, "It's best not to be inspired in the first place if you don't have the practical tools to respond to the inspiration." He meant that what we needed was not the momentary flash of so-called 'enlightenment,' but the ability to take realistic measures that allow you to enjoy what you have seen and understood for the rest of your days. Besides, he would say, it isn't enlightenment we need, but intimacy with ourselves and others.

I appreciated Carrey's humor, not to mention his honesty, but I wanted to tell him not to worry about trying to 'get back there.' What he had felt was only meant to be a one-time thing, anyway. Such experiences are given to us to understand that we are in the natural state—that everything is indeed the power of life happening, even if we don't experience it all the time. My teacher would say that once you understand something, you don't need to carry it around all the time. You don't have to keep lugging it around everywhere you go. He kept repeating that what we need is a practical response to that insight—a way to enjoy our natural state without setting up this struggle in the mind to re-experience something. We need action that works, not just wishful thinking or heroic efforts in the mind or body.

The point is that you cannot make permanent peace happen. Looking for it implies its absence, so the looking is itself the problem. Setting up the social model of enlightenment only creates un-enlightenment and devalues our ordinary lives. Only unhappiness looks for happiness! If happiness comes, it comes naturally and spontaneously. In the meantime, we need a response to grace. In the tradition from which sages such as Ramana appear (someone unobstructed in body or mind from the power of creation) the response is to be intimate with your own life, and all conditions of your life. This is how we respond to those moments in our life when we feel uncomplicated and free, whether they come as meeting a person like Ramana, as a shamanic experience, a love affair, or a life-changing experience in nature. Without a practical way to respond, we will slot these encounters into our socialized assumption of 'higher' and 'lower' experiences, and like Jim Carrey, we will go looking for more highs. Grace will make us even more miserable as we produce a painful split from our apparently mundane lives. The practice of intimacy allows for direct participation in the relationship and all conditions, not seeking-based contemplation, social disempowerment, and life-denial. Spiritual life is about participation in God, not the search for God. We do not need to deny Sex, the body, and the world in a hunt for God. Immersion in the union of opposites, which is all of life, reveals the heart that sages such as Ramana pointed to. This is how we keep safe with saints, sages, and realizations of all kinds.

Attempts at realization via religious ascent or contemplative projects are both futile and have contributed to patriarchal misogyny, the denial of the feminine. In fact, the source heart and its flow, which we could call God, are realized in complete integration or embrace of all ordinary conditions, all opposites—including, of course, sexual union, the principle human experience and function (in all forms of sexual orientation). But I want to make it clear that the perfect harmony of opposites in the natural state is available to all, with or without sexual practice. 'Sex' is simply the convergence of opposites and so can be felt by all. I assure everyone that you can enjoy this reality in a normal life.

The heart is the place of perfect giving and receiving, and any practices we might choose to do are not efforts to 'open the heart' as if it is not already flowing, but simply the perfect participation in this giving and receiving (masculine and feminine), within and without, allowing the heart to be felt and the nurturing force of life to move in an unobstructed flow. This flow is life. It is nature. And it is Sex. Inhalation sacrificed to exhalation and vice versa—the eternal strength of life that is utterly receptive—is the principle means of restoring the natural state. Then Heart/God/Source can be enjoyed and transmitted. It is easy and it is for everyone; it is relevant both to the entire religious tradition of humanity and to everyone here in the post-religious age.

Genuine spiritual practice is participation in the union of opposites. It is making love with life, and this extends naturally to another person. It is not the denial of Sex in the search for God, and it is not the exploitation of Sex in the search for God. Participation in the given must be there, otherwise spirituality is a hit-and-miss affair in the psychology of extreme spiritual attainment. Even the 'hit' creates misery, because for every high there is a low, which becomes the predominant context of the highs. There must be a steady practice of intimate connection and response to grace.

Sex is no more and no less than participation in this intrinsic union, which is the nurturing force and generative means of all forms of life (literally!) and everybody's birthright However, patriarchal dissociation has toxified human sexual intimacy, creating dreadful pain we are only just beginning to investigate. With immense sympathy to all of us who have inherited the burden of patriarchy, we don't have to do this escape attempt any more. We can participate again in the inherent union of strength and receptivity, so one empowers the other in endless mutual exchange, just as it is in the natural state. Let us practice our hearts out as participation in the union of opposites within and without. Let us reclaim our lives by getting through the valid stages of emotion: fear, anger, pain, and grief. Let us not get stuck at any stage, and come instead to grief for the dreadful social circumstance passed on to us. From grief, the powers of compassion spontaneously arise for all, and with them the ability to receive each other and experience the peace and power of the heart's flow in the natural state.

## CHAPTER FIFTEEN

# *The Validity of Desire*

*People rail against the passions, without dreaming that it is with its torch that philosophy lights its own*

—Marquis de Sade, *Histoire de Juliette*

*The lie that we each carry can be dissolved only by doing exactly what we want to do, without qualm or hesitation. May your desires wipe out whatever lies remain here, and efface the grand inquisitor from your brain.*

—Raoul Vaneigem

"WHAT DO YOU WANT?" MY DEAR FRIEND U.G. KRISHNAMURTI used to say to his friends around him, "What do you really want?" Rather than getting spiritual in pointless seeking towards castles in the sky, you can settle into your life and realize that you *can* have what you really want—complete intimacy on a daily basis, whether you are in a relationship with a beloved or not. You can make love with life every day. That is the highest pleasure. And the pleasure pathways are the spirit pathways! Please give up the absurd separation between God and Sex that has seen our ordinary desires made complicated and repressed. The legacy of religious doctrine has produced a distrust of our impulses, because true desire is rooted in the body—and therefore has been seen as unreliable and out of control, like a wild animal is presumed to be. Through imagining a separation of God and Sex, the womanless men of orthodoxy made cultures in which the intelligence of the whole body is shunned in favor of a 'higher' intelligence of mind and spirit. Lust—the natural chemistry of attraction between intimates—has been repressed and demonized rather than revered as the motive force of God. It is not even understood as an intelligence at all, and is confused with forms of contrived social greed. We still carry this legacy around with us. So-called 'higher' callings beckon us away from our instincts and we are easily led down fruitless paths. When the question is asked, "What do you *really* want," it is meant to help you distinguish between your true natural desires and the contrived desires put in you by the society you were born into. For example, the desire for sugar and deep-fried carbohydrates, or the desire for the female form without hair or curves. Or, the desire for God, as if God could be absent from your own breath, from your own life, from your own Sex.

Intimate connection is the principle desire of a sane life. We intuitively understand this already. The desire for intimate connection expresses itself in all of us, regardless of our belief systems. We want to be intimate with ourselves: to feel at home with our own body and breath. We want to be intimate with the wonder of our musculature and the astonishing mystery of our brains, in which there are more neurons than there are stars in the Milky Way. We want to be intimate with others, especially a sexual partner. This is the point of life. Right here, in our own communities, is the complete, inexhaustible mystery of the cosmos. And we want to be intimate with the infinite—whether we express this desire as the desire for God, Nature, Life, what-have-you. Every day we all seek ways to break down barriers between us. We see the disastrous effects when connection and intimacy are denied: look at the effects of solitary confinement on prisoners, or the effects of isolation on the happiness and health of the elderly. Or what happens when young men are confined as priests in monasteries and then later let loose on the public without any embodied intimacy in their life. Our sense of identity and self-worth and the values we come to hold all grow out of our relationships. We are social mammals. The importance of our interdependence cannot be overstated.

We all want to enjoy our relationships more fully. Yet modern lifestyles are so oriented towards education, work, achievement, and material success that taking time to relate and relax into Life with ourselves and with one another is seen as a secondary consideration, rather than life's most fundamental activity. Without intimacy as their principle, the social imperatives of religion, career, consumerism, politics, art, and everything else become at best unsatisfying, and at worst aberrant social struggles that deny and even suppress the natural human need for intimacy and sexual union. Our culture has not served us well.

I have a friend who rang me up a year ago in a state of deep distress. After years of overwork, he had been forced to leave his job as a high-flying lawyer following a public meltdown during a meeting. With no choice but to slow down and rest, he told me that he was struggling with his new situation in life. He was used to spending his days working in the city, moving nimbly between clients, exercising his intellect under pressure, and earning a big salary. He was a 'whizz-kid,' someone who seemed to have made it in life. You should have seen his suits. He liked the pace and challenge of his job and was probably always there late at night. The demands of the job and his attitude of taking everything on had pushed him beyond his physical and emotional limits. Feeling depressed, his doctor told him that he needed 'deep-rest.' He was forced to simply stop, but he told me that he didn't know how to do nothing. He said that after several months off work, he was feeling like he couldn't tell who he was anymore. Work had provided a sense of identity and a clear, daily routine. Now, sitting at home while his partner went off to her job, he found himself feeling anxious and lost. He didn't know what life was about anymore—what the point of it all was, and even if it was worth living.

This man was never given the tools to be intimate with his real desires. He had been plunged headfirst into the world of career and competition, and had lived a life based entirely on the principle of strength. Brought up to be a go-getter, he had been taught to penetrate the world and compete. I knew that he had absorbed a great deal of this pressure from his parents, middle-class professionals. He had taken up the mantle of their values and played them out in his own life without really choosing to. He didn't have an alternative framework for understanding what constituted a meaningful life. So it was no wonder that when he had to stop work and halt his career progression, he found himself feeling completely lost. When I asked him what he wanted, he panicked. He said he had no idea. He knew what society and his parents wanted from him, and he had become skilled at meeting those demands. But he had never been given the means to even consider his own desires. This young man's burnout was caused less by the stress of the job and more by the stress of constantly trying to meet the arbitrary standards of society and family. Eventually, his body declared that enough was enough. I told him that this was not a personal failing and that there was an extreme intelligence at work in his body's need for deep-rest and relief from a lifetime of struggle.

Over time, with rest and the gentle discipline of a short practice of movement and breath, my friend's system began to heal itself and return to a sense of vitality and energy. We met at his home, and I sat with him and his wife and could see significant changes in him and in their relationship. Several months after his initial crisis, he had come to feel that it was a chance to take stock of how he lived in the world and what he really wanted. Through the practice of participating in the polarities of strength receiving in his own body, he felt a greater desire to enjoy and embrace his relationship. In turn, his partner felt received as never before in the relationship. It was beautiful to see. The couple was discovering a depth of intimacy and love that was worth more than any job title could ever be. In our economies today, there is so much uncertainty and changing of careers that it is clear that to base a life simply on career and assets is not sufficient. We need an alternative way to live our lives and to value ourselves. And this way is about being intimate with life as it is, in every aspect. We are not educated in these matters. We are prepared for the factories and the universities, but not for life. It's time for action; it's time to change our value system and the deal we are dishing up to young people. How exciting that there is hope. There is hope for humanity.

Consumer society is not a wisdom culture, and it does not equip us to live our lives according to our ardent ordinary impulses. Many of us have been caught up in the drive to attain a sense of belonging through career pursuits. Others have reacted against this pressure by trying to drop out of the rat race entirely, moving somewhere difficult, or joining a spiritual community and building up identity around alternative lifestyle. Spiritual cults prey on those who crash out of the western drive towards career success, sucking up vulnerable people by posing as a genuine alternative to the alienation of modern culture. Yet these cults simply swap one race another; the secular rat race is traded for a spiritual rat race of arduous meditation and other feats towards the hoax of enlightenment.

I have another intelligent friend who had a successful career working towards a doctorate in art history. Brought up in an immigrant family that valued hard work and self-sacrifice, she had a sense that she owed it to her parents to push herself into a career in academia. Despite a deep reverence for her professors at the university, by the time she came to conclude her degree, she became paralyzed with fear. Right at the crucial moment, she found that she simply couldn't continue. On the verge of completing something she had devoted herself to for years, her mind gave up. The stakes had become too high. Regular pleasures and even dating had been sidelined while she focused on this undertaking. She told me that she used to just sit in her office on campus and stare at the screen, terrified that she might fail and let her family down, and yet unable to continue.

She told me that reading spiritual books had seemed to be a solution, as they spoke to the overwhelming pressure of competition and achievement that she was suffering from. Her reading led her to a community of people who were also critical of the constant drive towards secular success, and she eventually began travelling to Thailand, where a well-known guru was leading meditation retreats. My friend reported that she deeply relaxed on these retreats, and that when she sat with the guru she felt a sense of blissful surrender and absorption into life. All of her problems seemed to fall away, and others said the same thing. Aspirants left behind their secular identities, their career pursuits, and even their name. For the first time in her adult life she felt a sense of distance from the pressure she had put on herself. She told me that she felt like she had "come home to herself."

But when she left the retreat, she felt all of her familiar feelings of lack and anxiety return. Again, she was terrified. Before, she could blame university culture, but now, she felt like it was her own 'ego' and attachment to her individual identity that was preventing her from existing in a constant state of bliss like the guru. She believed that she needed to meditate more and would eventually be able to leave behind all worldly attachment and possibly even move to Thailand permanently. She gave up certain foods, stopped seeing her friends and family, and gave up Sex and avoided getting involved in any kind of intimate relationship. After a year of this rollercoaster of feeling occasionally blissful and mostly fearful, she happened to pick up my book, and came to realize that she was stuck in yet another high-stakes self-improvement program. She had left the university because she was trying to climb the academic hierarchy and attain a sense of belonging through achievement, qualifications, and impressing her professors. But in leaving her academic work, friends, and family behind and travelling to Thailand to 'be spiritual,' she had simply swapped one arduous project for another. She had traded secular progress for spiritual progress; academic 'knowers' for spiritual gurus; career progression for the hoax of enlightenment. I told her that if she really wanted to be spiritual, she should get a boyfriend or a girlfriend, because that's where the real spiritual fire happens. She did not need more achievements of any kind; she needed intimacy with body, breath, and relationship in that order.

Spiritual cults have a lot of answer for when it comes to making sincere aspirants who are looking for something different from the usual dysfunction feel ashamed of their very natural desire for attachment and relationship. The idea that 'needing' somebody is a symptom of your spiritual weakness; the idea that you need to give up the kind of commitment, dependence, and attachment that naturally arise out of love and intimate sexual union; the idea that asking your lover to commit themselves to you is unreasonable or 'clingy'; the idea that polyamory and 'non-attached' sex with multiple partners is valuable;

or the idea that Sex itself is unspiritual and must be transcended. These ideas are terrorism on ordinary people just looking to have a decent relationship. The fact is, we *are* attached to one another, we all come from one another, and we all need each other. We are as dependent on one another as we are on the sun. We are completely dependent on light, literal light received by 16 trillion cells. Without the sun, human life on Earth would cease in eight minutes. How finely tuned we are in this perfect harmony with the cosmos. It is exactly the same with each other. The separation of God and Sex presents solitary confinement (monastic renunciation) as the highest form of spiritual life. Turn around and go back!

We must engage sexual intimacy as the first principle of a sane life. It is within everybody's grasp as the natural form of life. The struggle with self and others ends when polarity, the form and process of Life, is engaged as a social priority both within and with another. It is the mutual accord that is valued above all else; the relationship itself is our priority and pleasure, of which sexuality is a vital part. Sexual character develops and everything else falls into place following on from this first principle of Life. Our life becomes informed and ordered by intimacy, intelligence, and power—including stable family and community life. Human contentment, wellness, wisdom, and realization lie in the power of mutuality between opposites, within and without, whether in same-sex or opposite-sex intimacy, in any gender identification or none.

It is almost impossible to work out what you really want, however, when your whole system has become tuned to what others want of you. Because we feel a sense of not belonging, we desperately try to meet the expectations of others in order to get a sense of belonging from them. Without tangible participation in life, the pressure is on the people around us to fill that hole. And the pressure is on us to perform in the ways that will hopefully keep them interested in us. It looks like difficulty talking about our real feelings and thoughts and difficulty being honest about what's really going on. Difficulty being real. Not even knowing what real might be. Not knowing what we want, because we get so tuned in to what others want, so they will love us. To discover our natural desires, we need to realize that connection is inherent, not something to be solicited from others. Then we can move and connect to others in the honesty of natural desire.

Many people, especially women, have been taught that sexuality is about being an object to be desired, rather than an actual person with desires of their own. As the embodiment of God and Sex, each person can come to feel that they are allowed to have agency and make choices for themselves, not just wait to be chosen. We gradually work out what is right for us in our own unique tastes and chemistries.

Social models passed on by parents usually express a limit to intimacy. Behaviors are duplicated automatically. There is a great deal of pain, difficulty, and plain awkwardness in our family lives because we all feel the weight of these limitations. Life is about understanding and releasing these limiting models through our tangible relationship with the unrestricted nature of Life. We discard the social obstructions passed through the generations but honor parents as the fundamental source of life. In this process, parents are to be forgiven for passing on their limits to us, for they too were dealt a bad hand. We are the first generation that can do this en masse, because the non-hierarchical practices of participation are now tangibly given from the great tradition in modern times. We have in our hands the tools to participate in our real desires and move through life on our own terms.

There may be a little experimentation required as you master desire. The simple practice of participation in the power of our life is the process of throwing out the limits we inherited from society and living in what is actually happening. We get to know ourselves and become capable of moving in our own chosen directions. So don't be afraid of desire. Use your God-given desires and learn which ones are truly yours and which ones have merely been put in you by orthodox mind. William Blake wrote, "He who desires but acts not creates pestilence," and "You never know what is enough unless you know what is more than enough." Desires become refined, pleasures become sweet and deep.

The desire for sexual union is the most powerful force there is. Mother Nature's only interest is for you to leave an improved version of yourself before you exit stage left. This is not to say that you need to engage in literal Sex or create a human being, but that's how powerful, intelligent, and unspeakably beautiful Sex is. Desire is real and beautiful. Lust is real and beautiful. Lust is God's method on Earth, the means of creation. Whether or not we choose to have a child, we can choose to engage this natural force in our life with another or by ourselves, in our feeling of the union of opposites within. Consumer society provides a vast inventory of substitutes for the intimacy that it itself obstructs—sugar and fats, alcohol and drugs, social struggles for imaginary power over others, cheap sexual thrills, and far-fetched projects of enlightenment. These celebrity-endorsed offerings are promoted as the bounty of civilization, even though they make us sick and distract us from what really matters. Don't fall for these consolation prizes. Don't give them a second thought. Focus on what really matters and what you really want. If you know what you want, no power in this world can stop you from having it. But if you want two things, you won't get either. You must get clear on what you want, and be real about it. And when you know what you want, know that you deserve it.

# CHAPTER SIXTEEN

# *Addiction*

*Man is free only when he is doing what the deepest self likes, and knowing what the deepest self likes, ah! that takes some diving.*

—Vivian Gornick

THE CAUSE OF ALL ADDICTION, WHETHER TO DRUGS, ALCOHOL, relationships, food, gambling, the internet, the hyperstimulation of our phones and technological entertainment, or anything else, is now recognized by some as having one source: (apparent) lack of connection, and the drive to escape the pain this has caused. And I don't just mean friendships and interpersonal 'connection,' but connection, intimacy, the whole-body knowing that whether with other people or alone, we are seamlessly part of the world, not a lonely bubble within it.* It is beginning to be understood that none of the things people commonly get addicted to are 'bad' in and of themselves; rather it is how we relate with anything at all that determines if we have a free or toxic relationship with it. I have met people suffering from insidious and crippling addictions to *samadhi* (bliss)! We use the word addiction

* And we could note that without this understanding, attempts to 'connect' with other people are not going to go very well, as they will be a desperate search to get a feeling from others that is already priorly given. This is why I recommend developing intimacy with body, breath, and relationship... in that order.

to describe a quality of relationship where we feel our ability for autonomous choice impaired in a compulsive hunt for temporary pleasure.

Almost everyone has been deprived of their sense of intimacy in Life, the primary pleasure, and so we all have addictions of some kind. Everyone has some degree of trauma obstructing their ability to be in the body and feel. The drive to escape our pain is the accidental drive to escape feeling altogether, and therefore deprives us of the means to feel connection, which then generates more pain. Try as we might, we cannot escape the suffering body, and every attempt to get away only creates more suffering. This is the cycle of addiction. The cycle cannot be broken through willpower; we must go in the opposite direction and address the underlying need that is trying to be met. Our own attempts to feel better are essentially valid, even if they have been misguided or destructive. Addiction is inevitable in a society in which God is assumed (and then felt) to be separate from Sex. Our already-established union with the all in all is denied and then repackaged as a union that must be attained.

We tend to associate addiction with the high-profile substances like drugs and alcohol. But it is a universal experience, differing only in the degree of social acceptability of what we happen to become addicted to, and the degree of urgency with which we pursue it. Most forms of addiction are so normal they are invisible, such as addiction to work, pizza, online shopping, gymnastic yoga, or Instagram. We are fish swimming in an ocean of addictive behavior! And some widespread addictions fly completely under the radar, like the addiction to our own internal chemistries while in certain negative thought patterns. Or the addiction to searching for God. What exactly we become addicted to is less important than understanding what we're really looking for, although it is useful to release any sense of shame or stigma that is still attached to particular addictions over and against any other particular ones. Some are more obviously harmful to the body-mind, but the underlying logic is the same. Popular culture and priests alike sold us separation, and so it was very normal and natural to go looking for a feeling of connection, and not our fault that the methods available were dangerous and toxic. Addiction expert Gabor Maté charts how the brain circuits and neurochemistries are exactly the same for all addictions, as well as the emotional dynamics of denial, shame, or secrecy. So there is no need to demonize those suffering particular addictions as different in any way from everybody else. There is no fundamental difference between the heroin addict and the monk who is searching for God. Both are trying to 'get high,' having been convinced that they are somewhere low. Looking for a connection that is not absent, both further obscure their ability to notice what is already present. We're all in it together.

The great psychologist Carl Jung once observed that a man's "craving for alcohol was the equivalent, on a low level, of the spiritual thirst of our being for wholeness… the union with God." Jung recognized that the compulsive need for alcohol was driven by the same search underpinning the world religions—but he doesn't seem to have noticed that the search for God is just as addictive and dysfunctional an activity as the craving to drink. What are we, if not already whole? The union occurred when our first cell came into being, and the socially implanted distinction between low and high stops us from noticing. And so trying to get to intimacy through addictive searching of any kind fails. It is looking for love in all the wrong places, and reinforcing the sense of separation it attempts to address. The experience of intimacy comes through feeling all there is to feel. Once we understand our search for connection and cognize that it is already the ecological truth for all of us, we can get serious about our conscious participation in it. Only through having the courage to feel the pain we are running from can we get what we really want, which is besotted intimacy with ourselves, others, and the entire cosmos. It is our birthright to come home into our bodies and enjoy the wholeness that is our situation.

And so, we can say that the movement of addiction is still an expression of Life's deepest intelligence. The root meaning of the word 'addict' comes from a Latin word meaning: "To dedicate or devote (one's body, mind, talents, *et cetera*) to an occupation, activity, or object." In this sense, addictive behavior expresses a desire for our lives to be organized in a meaningful, sustained direction. What this suggests is that we don't need to overcome our desires, but listen to them more deeply. "More, more, is the cry of a mistaken soul," wrote William Blake. But then he adds, "Less than all cannot satisfy man." So the problem is not that we are an addict, but that we are not addicted enough, or to the right things. Let us be addicted to infinity, addicted to endless depth of feeling, hopelessly addicted to making love with Life in our own beautiful form through the merge of the inhale and the exhale. Addictive behavior expresses a longing to be relieved of our limited social ideas and give ourselves over to the power of Life. But only as a power that *is* us, not as a power that is outside of us or above us. The latter is the usual social dynamic of disempowerment and leaves us as helpless children, hoping to be rescued and neglecting to rescue ourselves and each other. It is through feeling ourselves to be nothing other than this larger force that we come to grow and release limiting patterns. I offer my deepest sympathies to those who feel themselves to be in the grip of substances or unhealthy behaviors and I honor your urge to escape from pain and your search for connection. You have been served up a shoddy deal by your society, but it is within your grasp now to fulfil your real desires and step gracefully out of the cycles of addiction.

I have met many people who have been encouraged to identify as 'addicts' or as a person with an 'addictive personality.' They have found that the acknowledgement that one is addicted and not living safely serves a useful emergency purpose, preventing relapse and keeping them vigilant. Yet to take on the identity that you are an 'addict' is a trap, creating stasis rather than healthy growth. Whether in the depths of addictive behavior or in recovery, you are still the power of the cosmos, the absolute condition of reality. In sincere friendship I encourage you to participate in this eternal nurturing force and to move beyond your imagined limitations. We need not take on this identity as a permanent feature of our self-image or as something that differentiates us from others. Through the pleasure of participating in the given reality of the breath, the body, and all forms of tangible relatedness, healing and movement away from negative patterns occur naturally. Sometimes we replace negative patterns with positive patterns, only to eventually release all patterns and addictions altogether.

A very basic daily practice of moving and breathing allows us to feel our inherent connection, our aliveness. It happens naturally, so we don't need to be in a battle with our own cup of coffee. We find deeper pleasures that replace our existing addictive behaviors, which are only addictive because they are so inherently unsatisfying. We have to go back for another piece of cake, because the first piece stopped working! The practice of intimacy with your body and breath refines your pleasures. You might find you don't want a beer because it interrupts the refinement of the pleasure you are already enjoying: the flow of energy through the system, the felt connection to a friend, the palpable current of lust that moves between you and your lover.

We chuck out the false desires that have been put in us based on the false premise that we need to attain intimacy rather than participate in it. As we relax out of the search for God, Life hits us like a tonne of bricks. It is a nurturing power, an animating force that is happening as you whether you know it or not. No matter how chaotic your functional life may appear to be at this given time, you are completely looked after. Relationship is felt to be sublime and completely ordinary. This connection, this union, is what matters. The separation between God and Sex that runs through the world religions has glamourized the denial of pleasure, passion, and lust in the name of higher realities and left us searching. The denial of the natural pleasures of our own embodiment and relatedness produces the epidemic of addictive searching in the population. Hedonistic, unhealthy consumption is the flip side of the ascetic moralism of orthodox religion, the B-side of a broken record. To get our attention, spiritual practice has to be pleasurable, erotic in the most positive sense of the word. Otherwise we'll stick with our alternatives.

# CHAPTER SEVENTEEN

## *Sex is the Heart's Activity*

*Only from pleasures is born audacity and laughter, which rings out at orders and laws and limits; it will fall upon all who still judge, repress, calculate and govern, with the innocence of a child.*

—Raoul Vaneigem

I THINK WE CAN ADMIT THAT THE SEXUAL BEHAVIORS of the human species are terrible. They are afraid of their own Sex. Sex is Sex in all species, but other animals can have some bizarre sexual behaviors, and we don't have to compare ourselves with them. We are a refined animal—upright, built for receiving, with huge brain cores capable of receiving like nothing else we know in the universe. So sexually, it should be all about receiving. We have a fear of becoming like animals, and this fear dissociates us. The attempt to be more than human makes us less than animal.

Yet it must be said that Sex is completely natural. Just as your heart pumps blood through your veins and arteries, your body expresses an instinctive desire for sexual pleasure and intimacy. Sex is not some trifling matter to make philosophy out of, to exaggerate, to turn into a game, or to deny. Not a tool with which to manipulate one's own energy or another person's. Sex is the nurturing and regenerative power of nature. Human beings can feel and express their intrinsic union and shared life through sexual intimacy. Love is all about relating to another at a level that approaches identifying with that person. And because our bodies have soft, feeling skin, and strong, upright spines, we can express that love sexually.

You are permitted to enjoy the intrinsic power of Sex that constitutes the male-female polarity of your own system. Then, feeling the prior sexual fullness of your own biology, you can meet your chosen other in sexual embrace. Even amidst social dysfunction (the vulgar denial of Sex and the resulting vulgar exaggeration of Sex), you may enjoy what you already are and its power, pleasure, and purpose. The extremely intelligent beauty of life is functioning in you as you. Even the way your skin is functioning is extraordinary. And the intelligence of male-female polarity, which can create new life, is an unfathomable intelligence that science cannot fully comprehend. The practice of the polarities of your own embodiment is a catalyst that can naturally result in outer polarity and collaboration with another, whether in same-sex or opposite-sex intimacy. This may never be doubted. It is the natural order of things to love and be loved in the great power of life.

For most people, however, the wholeness of this expression is enmeshed in social expectations and mental limitation. The spiritual denial of Sex, the commercial distortion of Sex, and the pornographic exaggeration of Sex make up a wide spectrum of repression and dysfunction. The result is a lack of sensitivity and connection. Clearly, Sex deserves the utmost respect. But it seems like we can't even mention the word without implying something negative or sleazy. Dignity needs to be restored to this word. We need to bring honor to the power of sexual union/collaboration. Neither consumer society, nor temple religions, nor new-age spiritual leaders demonstrate any kind of wisdom or practical understanding around these matters. Instead they offer a gross perversion of the natural force of Sex.

We have inherited a great dysfunction. This dysfunction around Sex has arisen precisely because Sex is life's most powerful inborn force. It is as powerful as breath. We are all meeting this natural force as best we can. There is no rule book, no 'shoulds' or 'should nots,' and everyone's sexual journey deserves our tolerance and compassion.

From celibacy to Sex addiction, from abstinence to pornography, from repression to promiscuity, from casual hook-ups to crippling co-dependence, everyone is responding to the given situation of Sex within society's confused interpretation of it. Even criminal outbursts must be seen in the context of the social disease, and we must nurse and protect the abused first and then educate the abuser back to positive life. Through all of this, one thing is true: Sex is completely natural, and we can carve out a path of intimacy and sexual wisdom for ourselves *because* it is natural. Everyone can enjoy intimacy with life by connecting with the inherent sexuality of their own body and breath. Right now, you can experience intimacy with the male-female polarity that is in you. If Sex does not occur, it does not matter. Sex is already happening as the substance of reality.

Except that as a practice, it is increasingly *not* happening. Around the world, studies are reporting a 'Sex drought.' Young couples, older couples, single people—in many countries, people are having less Sex. This is not surprising when we consider the lackluster tension-release mechanism it is increasingly felt to be. The Sex people have been having is not special enough to be maintained in the age of smartphones, stress, exhaustion, and overwhelming life demands. We could hypothesize that as women become empowered, they no longer accept the male-centric Sex that has been the norm. They attempt to do something different, but the Sex remains curiously unsatisfying, because the deeper issue of domination of the feminine principle has not been addressed. We have not yet converted our sexuality into full-body loving, and so we are increasingly just not doing it at all.

The body loves its breath, and the exhalation loves the inhalation, and feeling this love tangibly allows us to love one another. When we feel loved, we inevitably give love to those around us. When we become intimately connected to each other from this place of mutual strength and receptivity, we are strong and present to each other as we receive each other. It is an endless eternal exchange. Sex is the heart's flow, a communication of love. It is easy and it is for everyone. Once you discover that the exhalation loves the inhalation as strength that is receiving, the male-female quality of life, you will immediately feel an uncommon pleasure in relationships. You will love your partner with an ardent connectedness, like we love our breath. Sex is no longer limited to the stress-release activity of the conventional orgasm, or something one ought to do but is just too tired for. You become more interested in fulfilling your partner by receiving their strength and movement. You become sensitive to one another in a sublime way.

From religious denial has come confusion, aberration, and illness around Sex. Globally, our already warped understanding of Sex has been made even more toxic by the burden of pornography, which creates the idea that Sex is a type of performance or fleshy stimulation, taking no account of the primal energy of reality that is exchanged between two people. Let us consider more closely the religious denial of Sex and how it has manifested, and how the modern exaggeration and exploitation of Sex is essentially the same activity—how both separate God from Sex. I'm sorry if it's all a bit depressing, but by understanding our context we can see how the pain and dysfunction we encounter in our lives and relationships are not our fault personally, but a fault of culture.

## CHAPTER EIGHTEEN

# *Sects Without Sex*

*The nakedness of woman is the work of God.*

—William Blake, *The Marriage of Heaven and Hell*

WE SHOULD BE ASKING OURSELVES WHY SO MANY INSPIRING religious figures have said 'All is God' and yet then wanted nothing to do with most of it—especially Sex. Just as the Indian saint Sri Ramakrishna spoke of "women and gold" as the obstacle to the spiritual progress of his devotees, it is a universal view that tangible conditions must be denied for the sake of some kind of intangible realization. What do we do with the fact that those who are most inspiring are also the most dissociated from sexuality? Do we try to emulate them? Do we write ourselves off as 'worldly' failures? Do we cynically write off the possibility of inspiration and just try and get by? When it comes to happy, healthy, sane, well-integrated sexual intimacy, our mentors have failed us—and that's without mentioning those who have been outright abusive.

The great beloveds of culture, such as the Abrahamic fathers, Buddha and Christ, Guru Nanak and Guru Ram Das, Rumi, Hafiz, and Kabir*—or in our own time, Bhagavan Nityananda, Anandamayi

* And innumerable other sages, women and men, forgotten by historical/cultural bias.

Ma, Sri Ramakrishna and Sri Sarada Devi, Ramana Maharshi, Jiddu Krishnamurti and U.G. Krishnamurti, Robert Adams, Thich Nhat Hanh, Sri Aurobindo and the Mother, Nisargadatta Maharaj, Neem Karoli Baba, Mata Amritanandamayi (Amma), and countless more, are to be placed in the context of whole-body relatedness with all conditions. We can love them all, not in the confinement of the traditions of transcendence in which they appeared but in actual tangible relationship. Forget the weight of culture that is telling everyone to transcend conditional reality and sexuality. We must go beyond these limits to really make use of our Buddhas and our Christs. There is only one reality arising in which everything is happening, including all saints and sages: my body and its relational dependence on the entire elemental world that is its context. My spouse, my guru, my deity, my god—the all is in all. What if the popes had had wives (or husbands) of equal status and visibility? Imagine what kind of civilization could have been built.

Deep intimacy with continuity is something that almost everyone secretly or openly longs for, or grieves that they seem to be unable to have, but we have been made to feel guilty about our incredibly natural desire for relationship by centuries of popes, priests, swamis, and internet gurus convincing the people that celibacy is spiritually superior (or else teaching 'non-attached' sexual exaggeration, which is the same denial of relationship—we'll get to that in later chapters). This ridiculous idea creates endless chaos in human life, from the extremes of abuse by Catholic priests to the everyday dysfunction suffered by regular people just trying to have a nice relationship. Only now can we re-cognize that God and Sex are (and always have been) one and the same thing and put an end to the madness.

Women's sexuality has been seen as such a threat to society and has been subject to paranoid control through ownership-based monogamy. The resulting social pressure to be in relationship—your grandmother grabbing your hand to see if there's a ring on it—produces the opposite social reaction of resentment and resistance to life's natural movement towards relationship. Women are sick of being aligned with Sex, and want a turn being aligned with God, and there are plenty of popes and swamis ready to seduce them into that. But true rebellion would be to break the artificial binary and be in reaction to nothing. We enter relationship with a person of our choice, not because our parents are pressuring us to, but because it is the enactment of God realization.

We have seen how dualistic religious thought structures that perceive the embodied world as devoid of spirit and therefore second to a higher spiritual plane create the religious denial of Sex. The motive-full renunciation of Sex is an insane religious thought structure imposing its will on the intelligence of nature and the body. The pursuit of 'higher' states of consciousness or spiritual transcendence denies the 'lower' body and its 'base' desires. This denial of Sex only causes serious pain and dysfunction. When you hold your breath for too long, you can't help but gasp for air when you inhale. In the same way, 'holding in' Sex will create aberration when it bursts out inappropriately. When you take Sex away from people in the search for transcendence, it inevitably comes out as an illness. Many famous, supposedly celibate guru personalities achieved worldwide fame, only for sex scandals to break the lie wide open. The more fervently such figures preached celibacy, the more likely that stories of sexually deviant or abusive behaviors would later surface. Our awareness of the scale of abuse of innocent children by Catholic priests continues to deepen. These priests were young men who had their life taken off them. They were denied the feminine. This is not to excuse criminal behavior, but to understand and address its root cause. Celibacy is not a measure of strength but an indication of confusion—namely, the mistaken belief that sexual practice somehow conflicts with spiritual realization. The pope is a fake pope without a popess (or an intimate fellow pope). There is no wisdom without the collaboration.

All of reality (including the body and Sex) must be embraced, not transcended or manipulated. There have been ancient cultures that were all about '*darsana*' or beholding: the body and its cosmos were all seen to be arising in and as the One reality. All was known to be God. There were no power structures of special access, no contemplative efforts, no ideas of future realization of God or enlightenment, only relationship—besotted intimacy with all. In such culture, it is our intimate relationship with anything and everything, especially our sexual intimacy, that allows us to feel the power of all arising conditions. We behold one another as the force of life.

## The Seduction Of Celibacy

The worst desire that has been put in us is the desire for desirelessness. This socially contrived desire leaves us eternally in conflict with our own natural movement towards intimacy and relationship. A very, very few eccentric individuals in history have accidentally found themselves in a state where there is no natural impulse towards Sex with another person, and from here it has become an ideal imposed on everybody else.

In society, there seem to be only two options. One is to have a lot of unfulfilling Sex, and when that fails, the other option on offer is to have no Sex—whether on purpose, sanctioned by religious idealism, or accidentally, due to there being no sexual wisdom or teachings on sexual intimacy available in our usual life. People usually oscillate between the two.

Fear of Sex, commodification of (female) virginity, and the remnants of patriarchal ownership models lead some into the temporary state of celibacy known as 'wait until you're married.' While it is a good idea to hold Sex as sacred activity, and while I respect all sincere religious practitioners, this choice is usually being made based on the belief that Sex is dangerous and/or for procreation only. If these social beliefs are present, it is not really a free choice. Sex is not something to be casually leapt into, but we are destined for disappointment if there is not some learning prior to making your choice in life partner. I encourage you to make your decisions, whatever they are, in a new framework, one that recognizes Sex as God's method on Earth. (Additionally, couples run into confused ambiguity when they begin to ask exactly what sexual acts they are and are not 'allowed' to do within this moral framework. It betrays the basic misconception that Sex is some specific physical act, rather than the mutual flow of energy between intimates.)

Please discard the absurd premise that you can have God or Sex but not both. It is simply not true. Sex and spirituality are one and the same and cannot be dissociated. I have facilitated men's groups that were full of young and older men who had experienced difficulty in their early sexual experiences and had then been seduced by the spiritual ideal of celibacy and the glamour of themselves in that choice. I have been stunned to hear these young sophisticates interested in spiritual life assume that they must make a choice, either God or Sex, and then struggle with the consequences. The subtitle of this book is 'now we get both.' By 'we,' I mean both all of humanity, and you personally with your chosen intimate partner. A vital consideration in these matters is that love and Sex are always an intimate affair. Love is personal. It is an appreciation of an actual person. Intimate relationships *are* the primary vehicle by which we experience and express our love. The idea that withdrawing your attention from physical intimacy with another person will somehow free up energy to focus on spiritual devotion or love of God or guru is misguided. Attempting to depersonalize your loving by placing it in a larger context, such as universal love of humanity, or love for God, will only succeed in watering it down. Where will you find God, exactly, if not in the person in front of you, despite their patterning and annoying habits? As our friend William Blake wrote, "God only acts and is, in existing beings." If you have an attraction towards universal or devotional love, the perfect place to learn how to express this is toward your intimate partner, not toward an abstract idea.

I have a young friend who confesses to having been in a dysfunctional wannabe 'spiritual' relationship for some years, in which both her and her partner expressed the belief that their relationship was of secondary importance to their relationship with 'Life.' Both sincere young people were trying hard not to be 'needy' or dependent, unconsciously playing out the avoidance of intimacy put into them by childhood patterning and negative experiences in previous relationships. The more they pulled away from each other in their attempt to transcend 'lesser' relationship, the more each felt wounded and became someone you would want to pull away from. They weren't given the alternative perspective to realize the obvious fact that the person in front of them *was* the power of the cosmos, the very form of God given to them to recognize and enjoy! This is what I mean when I say that the religious habit of seeing God as 'other' has trickled down into modern society and is messing up people's lives. In our discussions, I pointed out that her own form was the sacredness she intuitively valued, and showed her how to participate in this through a simple practice of breath and movement. My friend realized how silly it is to look for an abstract higher power, rather than prioritizing the relatedness with the people right in front of us. It is when we fully show up for our partners with commitment and continuity that we are able to enjoy a truly 'spiritual' relationship, if you want to use that word.

Perhaps you are someone who is thinking about renouncing Sex, because you have experienced how conventional relationship produces such emotional chaos, busyness of mind, and even depletion of energy, all of which may seem to obstruct our spiritual practice or secular life goals. Our cultural myths told through film, literature, and standardized humor are full of stories about how relationship obstructs or prevents great people from achieving their destiny. With great sympathy, I am saying that relationship is possible on different terms, and the desire to 'tap out' altogether, while very understandable, IS what has created the pain and dysfunction in the first place. Relationship itself is how we release emotion, find peace of mind, and regenerate our energy. If you want to contemplate God, get your Sex sorted, otherwise you're just going to be thinking about it all the time. So many people leave relationships or don't do relationships because they've seen their dysfunctions play out in their early experiments. The relationship has brought them face to face with their socially imposed limitations, and they hope to escape them by escaping relationship—perhaps to 'work on themselves' for a while. This is a mistake. It is better to practice intimacy with your own body and breath and gently move forward into the real spiritual work of healing humanity's dysfunction in your own case. Don't get spiritual. Know that your real spirituality is intimacy with all tangible conditions.

## CHAPTER NINETEEN

# *The Secular Train Wreck*

> **Train wreck** • *informal* a chaotic or disastrous situation that holds a ghoulish fascination for observers (OED)

JUST AS LOOKING FOR GOD IS A RIDICULOUS ACTIVITY, so too is looking for Sex. You are Sex! You are the force of life: your eyes perceiving these words, your mind connecting them with various thoughts and feelings, your hair growing, your heart beating. The body is a perfect and sublime intelligence. Sex is already complete in it. It is the beauty of existence. Why would you want to hunt for Sex in a desperate scramble when you already are that? Male and female are in perfect collaboration in your body—yet the norm is to either deny or exaggerate our Sex. Centuries of denigration of the tangible has created in us a search for higher realities, a struggle that literally numbs the body to its own inherent pleasure. From this disempowered situation, we go looking for pleasure in the train wreck of contemporary secular life. But it was here all along. Sex brings all life through and nurtures it; Sex is the nature of all animals, plants, and humans, but we live as if it is not. We make philosophy out of it and either repress or commodify it. Not receiving each other. On the one hand celibacy has been glamourized, but on the other hand of the same confused body are all sorts of sexual exaggerations, from pornography to 'neo-tantric' delusions, to the modern norm of casual sex devoid of intimacy. The denial of Sex and the exaggeration of Sex are basically the same activity: both assume Sex is something less than sacred based on the imaginary divide between God and Sex.

The underlying problem that Sex has been assumed to be something lesser is never addressed. This assumption, and the search for a missing God as if God is absent, has obstructed our ability to be intimately connected with ourselves and one another. No amount of creative new sexual arrangements or exploration will help if we don't end the abusive dynamic of dissociation happening right here in our own bodies that stops us noticing and feeling that Sex *is* God's activity. We are designed to empower each other in an endless mutual exchange, a sublime flow of energy between bodies who deeply adore and receive one another. Our nervous systems are still contracted, however, from the forceful struggle of trying to attain some eternal possibility, so we must learn receptivity to soften our forms to feel all that there is to feel. Sex changes as we become receptive from the brain core right through to the genitals, and that is where the big change for humanity will occur. A decision to consciously participate in this harmony (that we are) is required to turn that programing around. Please don't exaggerate your Sex in the same old religious assumption that your life is a problem and you have to use Sex as a tool to get some possibility for yourself. With great sympathy, I encourage you to step out of the cultural mess, take a deep breath, and choose to investigate intimacy with yourself and all of Life before re-engaging in sexual practice. Simply understanding how the game is rigged by the same old life-denying rules is a powerful step towards breaking free of the whole scene.

## It's Never 'Just Sex'

Sex is never just Sex. We are soft, feeling creatures, designed to enjoy Sex as the heart's activity. Far from breaking social taboos, casual hook-up culture represents an intensification of the reach of consumer ideology into our lives. Intimacy, friendship, and love are sidelined in favor of choice and casual, on-demand sex. Sexual freedom has been branded as the ability to move from one partner to another, engaging in transactional sex where no one has to commit to really investing their mind, body, emotions, or life with another person. As a cultural ideal, this obscures the way in which, without receptivity, we have become incapable of doing so. There is not much risk, but not much reward either. The secular reduction of Sex to something casual and the religious denial of Sex are two sides of the same vulgar coin. This uninspected assumption is still with us and has reduced sexuality among young (and older) people to an act that is very casual and unsatisfying ('friends with benefits'). It is time for a change, time for an education, because now you can indeed have both God and Sex.

Society threw out some of the repressive norms of religion and has thrown itself into a lot of casual sex, but that hasn't been truly fulfilling either. God was supposed by many to be made up or irrelevant (and as a mental concept, it was), so no one was watching, and everyone could be as naughty as they liked in an adolescent relationship of rebellion with the old rules. In the absence of the controlling parent, people gleefully leapt into all the 'forbidden' or 'sinful' activities—but they remained bound by the old system's definition of what was sinful. Put simply, *Sex is not what those who demonized it think it is.* So it's no good to simply reclaim it without radically examining what it actually is. Sex is sacred activity, the very means of creation, a sublime wonder and mystery. The aggressive exaggeration and performance of sexiness is no more than adolescent rebellion that betrays the Sex negativity still within us. We only need to rebel when we still believe in the authority of the parent. The pleasure of breaking a taboo is a very limited pleasure. We get a small adolescent thrill in our own daring independence, but we're still fundamentally reacting to an authority that never existed. It's not autonomy. You become an authority when you are at peace with all authorities.

I have a friend who was never allowed any sugar as a child. As an adult she went crazy, buying bags and bags of candy and chocolate. She would fall asleep in bed surrounded by sweets. Aside from the sugar, she got an addictive thrill from doing the thing that had been forbidden. She had a sense of being her own person. We met, and I gave her a simple practice of moving and breathing to help her feel her own autonomy as a life-form and enjoy the refined sweet pleasure of her breath. We discussed the possibility of her releasing her conflict with the voices of her parents in her head and with her own addiction. She began to feel how empowerment and freedom is being able to truly choose what is best for oneself, rather than being trapped in reaction to over-controlling parents and the internalization of them. She began to enjoy the pleasure of intimacy with her own embodiment and her own breath and not require the temporary high of rebelling against imaginary internal authorities.

In just the same way, casual sex and sexual exaggeration are fuelled by a sense of gleeful rebellion against moralistic Sex negativity and parental/societal fear and control of our youthful innocent sexuality. We are still lost in adolescent rebellion against the inner and outer voices of Sex negativity. Yet just as with my friend, true freedom comes from finding what we *really* want, not merely doing the opposite of what is ordained. There is nothing very interesting or radical in sexual extremes, no matter how taboo. We are mostly sick and bored of being gleeful teenagers, doing the things that the imaginary parental God figure said were bad. We're sick of being defined in reaction to a set of irrelevant and toxic ideas. We're bored and pained by loveless sex.

To heal the cultural division drawn between God and Sex, we need more than abandoning God and trying to 'get' Sex. We need to participate in the actual confluence of the two, not because anyone told us to or told us not to, but because that is what life is all about. We don't need to be angry ex-devotees of the pope any more. Or perhaps we are just sliding along on the momentum of normal western culture, not exactly enthused by contemporary sexual norms but unable to imagine anything different. It's time to grow up and have our own lives of whole-body intimacy with sublimity. It's not some big, daunting project, because that sublimity is already going on as our bodies and all of nature.

In fact, just as God's method on Earth is Sex, the method of love is Sex. But Sex is not love and not a way to get love. We are very confused as to the difference between Sex and love. Practicing Sex without love has become a phenomenon of modern humanity, and it is literally painful and useless activity. Suffering an apparent lack of love in our lives, we use Sex as a method to try and get love, as opposed to an expression of it. Engaging with another in this logic of 'getting' makes us feel needy and depleted, rather than restored and loved. We are social animals, mammals who huddle together. Human touch is our natural need. Deprived of that and not even loving our own bodies, we throw ourselves into casual sexing in an attempt to feel the intimacy that is our birthright. None of it works. We are grateful for anybody who shows a little bit of interest in us, even if they are only interested in possessing our bodies to try and feel something themselves. Society has not yet learned how to love with the whole body with continuity in daily life. But I want to assure you that this can be easily learned and easily practiced. I understand that people have suffered dreadfully in their search to be loved.

It's no good throwing yourself at someone else and hoping that love develops, although this is the norm. I would like to encourage you to wait to enter sexual union with another until you are sure that you love and are loved, like and are liked, lust and are lusted. This may sound conservative, but the alternative is loveless sex, which causes very real trauma in our soft animal bodies. Whether we feel it or are too numb, mindless 'just physical' sex creates emotional pain we will have to unravel sooner or later, because we are not 'just physical' beings. The entire phrase 'just physical' suggests a split between the material and the mental/spiritual that just does not exist. As we come into relationship with the extraordinary natural phenomenon that we are, the irresistible impulse to be confirmed by another through Sex (regardless of their suitability) becomes less. Honoring ourselves, we become more capable of discernment and patience.

Of course, there is always a period of testing where we come together to see if a relationship can develop into true polarity. Chemistry requires experiments. Sex is not a dangerous force, but it is a holy one. It does not need to be controlled by religious or legal institutions, but it does need to be engaged in thoughtfully by self-respecting people. Not from any kind of moral judgement, but simply because otherwise we create unnecessary emotional pain for ourselves and others. Just turn on the TV and you are likely to see emotional chaos caused by a lack of sexual wisdom. Know that it is possible to carve a pathway for yourself in the midst of the chaos. Claim your own life of besotted intimacy.

### Polyamory

Many of us rightly reject the model of relationship provided to us by our parents, which tends to be monogamous (in theory) and something less than besotted intimacy. We want something more than the conventional 'two people in a box' model. So we go looking in the creativity of cultural options. But the emotional demands and absence of intimacy and sex in the average relationship are not a *result* of monogamy, but rather stem from a cultural fault that affects all forms of relationship. Just as the problem with pornography is not that it is sexual, but that it is violent and insincere, the problem with conventional relationship is not the monogamy but the inability to receive one another with depth of intimacy. Changing the arrangement of the relationship does not get at the underlying barriers to love that our culture has put in us. Believing that our bodies are beasts of burden that need to be bullied towards a distant ideal, we have whipped ourselves along until our tender nervous systems become more or less incapable of receiving. We don't need the proliferation of different social models, arrangements, and 'options'—we need a renewed intimacy with our own life, body, and breath. And then perhaps with a chosen other.

In our current culture of life-denial and intimacy-avoidance, the idea that we can have multiple partners is used to avoid the fire of mutuality between people, rather than to facilitate it. As our beloved Joni Mitchell writes:

> I recently read an article in Esquire magazine called 'The End of Sex,' that said something that struck me as very true. It said: "If you want endless repetition, see a lot of different people. If you want infinite variety, stay with one." What happens when you date is you run all your best moves and tell all your best stories.
>
> You can't do that with a longtime mate because he knows all that old material. With a long relationship, things die then are rekindled, and that shared process of rebirth deepens the love.

> It's hard work, though, and a lot of people run at the first sign of trouble. You're with this person, and suddenly you look like an asshole to them or they look like an asshole to you—it's unpleasant, but if you can get through it you get closer and you learn a way of loving that's different from the neurotic love enshrined in movies. It's warmer and has more padding to it.

Beware, because due to the failures of monogamy, polyamory is now politicized as a 'something', as some kind of legitimate alternative.* But it does not address the problems that have toxified monogamy. Polyamory is usually another form of patriarchy, controlling women. Adherents will often insist that more love is a good thing—but as we have discussed, Sex is not love. We love trees, but we don't go around trying to have Sex with them all. There are very valid criticisms to make of conventional monogamy, but they are not the fault of the form itself, and don't require us to reactively throw out the form. Toxic jealousy, for example, to which polyamory is presented as a solution, naturally dissolves when we come into continuity of loving, when we are lapping the nectar of our lover's energy, not by endlessly discussing, self-analyzing, or by forcing oneself into such overwhelming scenarios that we dissociate from relatedness. (Furthermore, some degree of jealousy can be natural and non-destructive.) People do not want to put their whole heart into someone who may not actually be available, and so there is a loss of intensity for everyone. I have met many women (and some men) who have been made to feel bad about themselves for being miserable within polyamorous experiments. Not only did they have a partner who was unable to perceive their limitless depths, they were also struggling with the belief that their pain meant they were a less spiritual, less enlightened, and less open and loving person. When a person (male or female) can't find the juice of real relatedness, they go sideways, trying another and another, never discovering the depth that you can go to in complete intimacy with life with another person.

---

* And even justified with studies of primate behavior, ignoring the fact that we are not ancient primates, we are modern bodies in a modern culture, with a unique (yet under-utilized) ability to stand upright and receive each other through the soft fronts of our bodies.

Monogamous continuity is the form in which you can get to that place of complete abiding where one empowers the other. There are more important things to do in life than to be endlessly discussing and processing emotional torment caused by complicated, messy arrangements. And just because you *can* handle it, doesn't mean you should have to. Polyamory may hold some appeal while we are still searching to be constantly affirmed by another person's attention, because it enables a person to be affirmed by more people's attention. But real relationship is about giving and receiving in an endless mutual exchange, two autonomous individuals who choose to be together in order to express love with the whole body, not about trying to 'get love' in an enactment of unfulfilled parent-child dynamics. God is not absent. Love is not absent. Existence is a vast interwoven harmony and dependence of all things with all things. That is love. Existence is love. We don't need to get it from anybody, because it is freely given and the looking for it is implying its absence. *'Stop looking, start living!'*

### Pornography

In secular society, our understanding of Sex has been made toxic by the burden of pornography, which creates the idea that Sex is a type of performance or is merely physical stimulation—'getting off.' The multi-billion-dollar industry of pornography and sexualized advertising provides a model of Sex that takes no account of intimacy or the primal exchange of energy that is shared between people. Instead, it creates a barrier between lovers by introducing image-based patriarchal standards of performative sexiness which are only an imposition on the natural instincts of the body and mind.

The conventional (or at least stated) distaste for pornography is usually based on an objection to Sex, rather than an objection to how pornography is unfeeling, misogynistic, and increasingly violent. The taboos that remain around sexuality (as the apparent opposite of 'God') mean pornography is judged for the wrong reasons. Our objection to pornography is not a moral one but a practical one: it just doesn't work in terms of giving people what they really need and therefore serves no purpose at all. Pornography separates sex from intimacy, and it is intimacy that we need. Like casual sex, it has arisen only as a reaction to the denial of Sex that has been society's norm until recent decades. Innocent young people wanting to receive a sexual education and feel something amidst teenage difficulties turn to pornography with all their youthful energy, innocence, and harmless interest in Sex. At increasingly young ages, this interest is exploited and perverted by infinite quantities of accessible, demeaning, violent, exaggerated, but mostly just unfeeling pornography. The more is consumed, the more tense and shut down their nervous system becomes, and the more they need to replicate similar dynamics in order to feel anything. Young men, innocently educated to think 'that's how Sex should go,' and simultaneously taught to contract their emotional sensitivity in order to be 'real men,' believe that women want to be slapped, dominated, or aggressively penetrated. The invisible lesson of pornography is that no sense of love or affection is required to satisfy a partner. Young women unconsciously learn to 'perform' Sex, tailoring their actions, noises, and entire 'performance' around the perceived desires of their partner. The social dynamic teaches them to be desired, rather than to desire, and so they may not even know whether they are autonomously attracted to their partner. Unfeeling and aggressive sex will only serve to further numb the body's capability to feel its own autonomous desires and preferences. Pornography is where teenagers are getting their sexual education, and they are hurting each other. We throw young people into college dorms, their hormones are raging, we ply them with alcohol, and we ask them to get on and do something about Sex. In most cases, they spend the rest of their lives trying to get over the pain they suffer in these early sexual failures. Or, we throw young couples into boxes in the suburbs and ask them to have Sex and have children, leading to pain and domestic disaster.

Performative sex results in a phenomenon known as 'spectatoring,' where a person feels dissociated from their own authentic feeling in their body and may feel a lonely sense of watching themselves from the outside. It's no coincidence such dissociation also occurs in situations of trauma or abuse. This is not a personal failing, but a natural and logical reaction to the inescapable social programing. It is the mind protecting us by distancing us from the unpleasant, unfeeling physical situation. Performing sexiness is the most unsexy thing we can do, as the performance lifts us out of our own authentic current of life and into a mind-imposed version of how we think Sex should look. We must get ourselves out of these situations and then learn to bring our awareness back into our bodies once they are safe. There will be much to feel and release as we do so.

Our culture of pornography is not limited to explicit sexual content but extends more broadly into media-driven sexual imagery everywhere we look. When people are overstimulated or exclusively stimulated by media-contrived images of sexiness, they lose their ability to be stimulated by actual potential intimates. Their idea of what they are attracted to becomes warped towards the social ideal and they become curiously unstimulated by the true energies of interaction. It becomes more difficult to find a relationship when attraction can only be felt towards a very few (not necessarily appropriate) people who fit the current visual ideal. All performative imposition of society must leave your intimate relationship for God and Sex to be felt as one. This can happen if you commit your life to being intimate with life—to your body, its breath, and all its natural relatedness. Aliveness becomes the most attractive quality, rather than the pornographic ideals of culture.

I deeply sympathize with all young people seeking to find a sexual education and intimacy through the mediums of so-called 'adult' magazines or online pornography. In its embarrassment and shame, your society has failed to give you more healthy channels of initiation and education. Feel no shame about your consumption of pornography—there is nothing wrong with your beautiful and healthy impulse to explore sexuality, but look elsewhere. I urge all young people to not worry about 'being good at Sex' but simply discover intimacy within yourself and then patiently look out for another person whom you really like, love, and lust ('the three Ls') and whom you can be yourself with. Tenderly and gently experiment together in sacred occasions of exploration and mutual respect and trust. Sex is not a skill set you have to master with bravado and technique, but a great spontaneous flow of energy between two people who truly care for one another.

And for all of us survivors of the social disaster, great sympathy for any shame we might have inherited from our dysfunctional societies. The cultural assumption that where God is, Sex is not, and where Sex is, God is not, has made a big mess for everyone that we have scarcely begun to understand. Trying to be something you are not *is* suffering, and nowhere more so than in sexual embrace, where real erotic energy can only flow in total honesty and authenticity. True and honest sexual intimacy is the greatest pleasure of all and makes redundant all the addictive pleasures society has come up with as a substitute.

## Neo-Tantra

At numerous commercial retreats in tropical countries around the world, schools and teachers are selling 'neo-tantra'—sexual exaggeration without a basis in actual practice of intimacy with our own breath and experience. (And often without any relation to the actual Indian spiritual tradition of Tantra either.) These schools make money from people's desperation around Sex, promoting an exaggerated, depersonalized understanding of Sex which removes sincere personal love from the equation and encourages individuals to use each other to achieve fetishized energetic states. Sincere people come to such places looking for alternatives to conventional, 'stress-release' Sex, and while they may find some increased capacity for physical pleasure, it is within an insidious instrumentalized view of Sex that treats your own body and that of your partner as a way to feel something, within the same familiar struggle of trying to get somewhere as if we are not somewhere.

Sex is not a technique to move energy or break down blockages in the body. It is because we love someone, and we bodily communicate that. Then, in the flow of intimacy, any blockages in our emotions and energy can gradually clear. In relationship, the body's energy* moves with its own intelligence. There is just no point trying to create some kind of idealized exaggeration of Sex through techniques. The very idea of using conscientious or clever sexual techniques reduces the one area of life that is allowed to exist just for its own sake to a mechanical

---

* Referred to in various traditions as *prana* or *chi* (life energy). Please note this is flowing *as* us, not through us. Otherwise, what would the rest be?

means to an end. Instead of "I love you," young (and older) people are finding ways to avoid the fire of vulnerable confession of love by saying, "Do you want to practice together?" Sex must not, cannot, be reduced to a project to feel something via the vehicle of another. It is *participation* in the union of opposites—the perfect intrinsic union of male and female that is all of life. There is no getting to it, because we are it. Rather than gymnastic, energetic, sexual, or any other kind of exaggeration, authentic Sex is simply participation in the given reality, a process of truly feeling and receiving ourselves and one another in an intoxicating endless flow. Only then does the nervous system uncurl. We discover the endless depth of feeling flowing within our own system and that of our beloved. Such love moves energy in torrents, beyond what any effortful technique could hope to achieve.

***

Sex is not a game, a stimulating entertainment, a search, a distraction, or a tension-release mechanism. It is a communication of love, a deeply sacred and private affair between two individuals. Only when we relax into the fact that God and Sex were never separate does honest and deep relationship become possible. We heal the primal knot caused by our dysfunctional inheritance. It becomes obvious that we are the power of life, arising as beauty and harmony. We need this basic re-wiring before we can hope to recognize this of another and overlook their social patterning—their imagined limitations, the dramatization of which is the usual relationship. First we come into intimacy of feeling with ourselves, then we are able to relate to others on this basis, forming relationship heart to heart rather than mind to junk-filled mind. We learn to relate in a feeling way and bypass the social mess. Through intimacy with body and breath, we relax and resensitize the body so it can truly love another, rather than just using other people and our own bodies to try and feel tension release, subtle energies, or attain temporary states of bliss. Sensitivity to our own embodiment naturally gives us sensitivity to another's and prevents us from instrumentalizing either one.

## CHAPTER TWENTY

# *Masculine Dignity: Strength Receiving*

*You do not have to be good.*
*You do not have to walk on your knees*
*For a hundred miles through the desert, repenting*
*You only have to let the soft animal of your body*
*love what it loves.*
—Mary Oliver, 'Wild Geese'

Masculinity as we know it is in a state of crisis. We have been handed a history of patriarchy and misogyny, cultural norms that have caused great pain and dysfunction for everyone. This crisis is being brought out into the open for serious public dialogue and it is about time. We are given plenty of information about the behavior of the worst abusers, and analysis of why it's harmful. There is even some recognition that men like them are obvious and particularly baneful examples of an issue that runs right through society and affects us all, rather than individual moral failures.

What is missing from the discussion, however, is a deeper understanding of *why* we are facing this failure of the masculine in the present world and of what we can proactively do to heal and move forward. We urgently need a new masculinity, one based on collaboration and intimacy rather than disconnection and abuse, and we need the means to make this a reality rather than a nice idea.

What underlies these destructive forms of masculinity? It is the same familiar systemic denial and abuse of the feminine—the whole open, receptive, wild, embodied, creative force of life. We avoid any kind of 'men versus women' debate by restating that masculine and feminine are just words to describe two forces that exist everywhere in mutual polarity, like the positive and negative forces within every atom. Not words to reinforce made-up gender norms. We all have both within us. We all come from mother and father, and all of us contain the male-female equation of life in perfect union, no matter our sex or gender identity on the male-female spectrum of Mother Nature's biologies. We all have a strong upright spine and a soft receptive frontal line and crown. We all embody strength that is utterly receptive. So talking about a 'crisis in masculinity' is not only pointing to an attitude problem in men. The problem is humanity's habit of associating masculinity with men and femininity with women and then valuing the masculine over the feminine, resulting in a big mess all round.

Young men are taught that emotion is weak and receptivity is unmanly, that the correct approach to life is one of hard aggression, and that intimacy can only be gained through manipulation, ownership, and control of the feminine. Masculinity defined and enforced like this deprives men of receptivity and real intimacy. Men have been dispossessed of the intimacy with the feminine (within and without) that it is their birthright to feel. They have had their emotional lives taken off them. The abused becomes the abuser. Sexual assault and other forms of dysfunctional sexual behavior all stem from this denial of the feminine and the resulting desire to try and 'get' the feminine. There is a deep drive to reunite with the feminine (within and without, whether in same-sex or opposite-sex intimacy). When this basic impulse is not given appropriate channels, it bursts out in every kind of inappropriate way. The male longing for his own feminine, his own wholeness, is projected outwards towards literal women. Women are controlled in the belief that they represent the only point of access to everything associated with the feminine that men have been deprived of: vulnerability, emotionality, softness, receptivity, and embodiment. When a person is not given the means to feel the power of their own life, which is already given and one hundred percent constant, all kinds of warped attitudes to Sex are created including the struggle to control it and get it. All along, it has been freely given as our own very nature. In the meantime, we must protect victims and educate predators, and that includes everyOne. It is urgent. Of course, there are many exceptions, but the common life still acts out these sad patterns.

To heal humanity from the pain that has been created, we must go beyond guilt, blame, and anger. We must grieve for the whole stupidity of the circumstance and have some compassion for ourselves and others. It takes courage to acknowledge just how numb and tuned out from ourselves, each other, and reality our culture has made us, whether or not this withdrawal has led to obvious abuse. We must all have the real courage to drop the bravado act that everything is ok. When men observe that they have accidentally duplicated the cultural denial of the feminine (within and without) that was imposed on them, they require the practical means to move in an entirely different direction. They need the tools to be free of the unconstructive anguish of guilt and the dissatisfaction felt at having been denied fulfilling intimacy.

This is where tangible practice comes in, the simple means whereby every person can learn to feel more and receive the great vital power of life that is exploding from the inside in themselves and everywhere. The ancient traditions offer us so much more than conceptual 'spiritual' games. Authentic intimacy with our own breath is strength receiving, participation in the union of opposites, male-female collaboration, and the power, intelligence and beauty of life itself. Through simple accessible movement coupled with breath, a visceral change in the body can occur. Men learn that strength with receptivity is more powerful than strength alone. It is a literal change in the nervous system as a person becomes able to receive their own experience and thereby becomes capable of tender and mutual intimacy with another. It is not about getting somewhere, but a remedial practice to remind us what is already here (albeit obscured by centuries of patriarchal dissociation). It is the birthright of every person to feel all that there is to feel; when a person is able to receive life in full feeling, sexuality will be real, true, honest, lawful, and the expression of love—the flow of the heart.

We could call this practical process of learning to receive the feminine 'the new feminism' (and the new masculine). It opens the door to relational collaboration as equals and opposites where one empowers the other in an endless mutual exchange. This is the generative, nurturing power of life itself, the very dynamic that is already alive as every body, regardless of sexual preference or gender identity.

The valid anger of earlier feminisms was a necessary and important survival mechanism that has paved the way for all women and men to be free. We can now observe, understand, and move quickly through all the necessary stages of emotion: numbness, fear, anger, the pain beneath the anger, and finally grief for the unnecessary circumstance imposed on all humanity. In grief, we receive the gifts of compassion and understanding and the ability to take a step forward in a new positive direction.

The pain has become undeniable. We have inherited a big mess, but we now have the knowledge and tools to tangibly participate in our lives, cut through the heavy layers of dysfunction, and restore sexual intimacy to its rightful place as a function of the heart. Through feeling and relatedness, we can return back to Earth and end humanity's violent struggle against the feminine. The masculine is restored to its natural peaceful power and dignity. The new measure of strength is how much you can receive.

CHAPTER TWENTY-ONE

# *Receptivity, the First Principle of Mutuality*

*The man [sees] the woman as a goddess,*
*The woman [sees] the man as a god.*
*By joining the diamond sceptre and lotus,*
*They should make offerings to each other.*
*There is no worship apart from this.*
—Candamaharosana Tantra*

IT SHOULD BE SO COMPLETELY OBVIOUS AS TO NOT NEED SAYING that any sexual intimacy should occur only in complete mutual enthusiasm. Bizarrely, it seems that this is not completely obvious to many, and so does need saying. Sex is the flow of mutual energies in an endless empowering circuit. Where there is not full autonomous enjoyment on either side, it becomes abusive, deadening, and a dreadful physical-genital stimulation only. I'm sorry to be crude, but it is masturbating in another person. In the extreme, this is sexual assault.

* English translation from Miranda Shaw, *Passionate Enlightenment,* Princeton University Press, 1994. Please forgive the heterosexual focus of this ancient text and know that the principle of turning intimacy into worship is relevant to all sexualities.

Prior to what we label as outright assault, we have a huge spectrum of unmutual, unfeeling sexual practice, where a person tries to just 'get' a sensation for themselves through the medium of another's body. It is a sign of our numbness that anyone is able to enjoy imposing such 'sex' on another, oblivious to or in disregard of their autonomy, let alone their pleasure.

The problem is that for thousands of years, both women and men have been taught a highly dysfunctional set of interrelated gender norms. These ideas of what was maleness and what was femaleness were not defined in isolation, but as intersecting parts of a closed system of patriarchal control of the feminine. For example, in all the major societies of the world, women have been taught that they are objects to be desired only, not allowed (or even capable of) their own autonomous desire. Even the existence of female desire has been denied, as it would imply that women are unruly human subjects, not mere biddable objects in the drama of the central male. (The paradox has always been that women are supposedly passive and lacking in desire and simultaneously so ravenous that they need to be subjected to constant control.) We have learned that Earth is not the center of the universe, but we have not yet fully learned that the male is not the center around which the woman should orbit. Autonomous female desire has always been a terrifying and destabilizing force to dominant powers of church and state, whose entire religious philosophy is grounded in denial, control, and attempted transcendence of the feminine. "[A]ll perish from the disorder of women," philosopher Jean Jacques Rousseau (1712–1778) wrote in *Politics and the Arts.* Handed from father to husband, traded for material wealth and objects, used as reproductive factories, legally owned by their husbands, married without a choice of partner, their virginity policed as a fragile commodity, women have been denied full personhood for a very long time. Social doctrine taught that they must passively wait to be approached by a man so as not to exhibit autonomous desire themselves. (Think about the conventions of dance, dating, or marriage to see how these ideas continue.) And even when approached, they were supposed to affect disinterest or even denial, because to admit active interest would make them dangerous and degraded desiring beings. "If women be formed to please and be subjected to man," wrote Rousseau in *Emile,* "it is her place, doubtless, to render herself agreeable to him, instead of challenging his passion." Women should display "that bashfulness and modesty with which nature hath armed the weak, in order to subdue the strong," he continues, in order to excite male desire and give men a sense of victory in conquest. His character of Sophie embodies such a woman, "made to please and to be subjugated." Looking back on these words from this leading philosopher of his time helps us understand how women have been taught to say 'no,' even while feeling 'yes,' and how men have been taught that they must override a woman's 'no' and assume that it probably means 'yes.' Women were culturally barred from being able to say an explicit 'yes,' because if they did so, they would be branded as sexually insatiable, lascivious whores. If our ancestors had not been trained to believe that 'no means yes,' then it is quite possible none of us would have been born. It is a deep legacy to turn around. Here in the age of individualism these dynamics continue, but without any way of understanding that our actions and thoughts have been inscribed into the social mind before we were even born. Do not feel bad if you ever found yourself unable to say 'no' when you wished or needed to. It was not your fault. Your options had already been limited by the society you were born into.

We must understand that we have literally been taught to avoid mutuality, because the flow of actual sexual current was associated with lust and therefore sin. John Gregory, the best-selling eighteenth-century European writer on young women's moral education, wrote that "violent love cannot subsist… for any time together, on both sides; otherwise the certain consequence… is satiety and disgust." In other words, if both partners feel lust/attraction toward one another, Sex becomes ungodly, but if one is a passive object, it is somehow okay. The actual sexual current of life was denied, even while some form of physical intercourse was happening. In the UK they used to say to a woman, "grit your teeth and think of England." We now call this sort of thinking 'rape culture'. It may seem like ancient idiocy, but the legacy of this sick cultural logic is still with us today. It is there any time a woman (or man) tunes out during Sex but feels the need to perform interest in order to fulfil a duty, any time a man (or woman) does not notice or respond to this lack of mutual feeling, any time a woman (or man) feels embarrassed of her own enjoyment of Sex, any time we are drawn to be with someone who we don't actually have a flow of chemistries with, any time we feel a sense of guilt or shame after being immersed in sexual pleasure.

The proposed solution has been to teach people to ask one another over and over again, 'are you into it, are you into it,' constantly checking for mutuality using verbal assurances. This strategy of 'consent education,' although an improvement, does not get to the root of the problem. We have to ask what has happened to a person who is incapable of feeling/noticing when their partner is not enthusiastically participating and who is even still able to 'enjoy' themselves. It shows we have a warped idea of what Sex is. When mutuality is not present, the flow of energy that is Sex is not present, so all that is left is physical stimulation. There needs to be a practical means to become completely receptive of each other as the primary principle of sexual intimacy. To be receptive is to be sensitive to another—literally, in our bodies, not just in our social ideas. In receptivity, love is the primary interest and mover. We begin to understand that there is *absolutely no pleasure at all* unless there is utter mutuality and receptivity. The point is that we give to each other in the context of receptivity. That is the practice of the heart. That is the flow of life and love between two good people. It doesn't need performance cues, technique, or words. These are coping strategies when our receptivity has been lost. The body knows what to do in the matter of giving and receiving. The human body is built for profound receptivity. Strength is *for* receptivity.

The cult of the normal is that woman is second to man. This goes through all strata of society and reaches into our personal relationships without us having consciously signed up for it. The usual Sex is organized around the male penetration and ejaculation. Women are conditioned to this arrangement and to measure themselves in how they fulfil this limited role. It is dissatisfying for all involved. Many people just give it up and stop having Sex, even while their relationships continue.

This book is an intervention to show everybody that there is a practical way forward to create mutuality in your life and your Sex and end the crippling patterns that our society is built upon. There may need to be a period of anger, pain, and grief as we come to terms with it all, but flowing from our grief is compassion and the practical healing means to be kind to yourself, your partner, and all others. We are living in terrible times, but there is great hope.

We have a new historical moment right now where women are bravely reporting their experiences of sexuality without receptivity and are being listened to. Amidst the usual denial and avoidance, some good men, young and old, are with shock receiving the news that there was not mutuality in their sexual experiments. Rather than wasting time in shame or guilt, this moment of soul searching can lead them to the realization that they have been deprived of receptivity, their bodies made oblivious to the experience of their partner. Men (and women) are now called to learn how to receive the feminine rather than dominate or exploit. And women (and men) are called to throw out the dreadful programing put upon them that women are subordinate to the male and "made to please," and therefore not allowed their own completely positive sexual experience. As Vivian Gornick writes, "the men are undone by the need to master, and the women by the power of self-doubt." When the two intersect, as they have been designed to, we have a situation of great pain. It is no one person's fault but a vast cultural predicament.

Receptivity is not a 'nice-to-have.' It is the essential quality that ensures Sex is actually Sex and not assault. Receptivity, the downwards current of life, brings us into our bodies, which is where we feel and commune with another. It is our natural state as children—consider how a child always knows when someone is upset—before we become numb in our bodies, and it is needed and possible for everyone. Without receptivity to what is already present, sexuality is misogyny: the pain of the usual experience. When we force the body's natural energy flows to fulfil social ideals, that is the domination of the feminine. Intimate participation in life is not an abstract teaching concept; it is the only way to ensure sexuality is real, honest, and mutual. Without understanding our Sex as nothing more than the participation in the already present reality and natural flow of life, sexual expression will be denied, forced, or otherwise become aberrant duplication of society's patterns.

# CHAPTER TWENTY-TWO

## *Right Relatedness*

*"The Self without sympathetic attachments is either a fiction or a lunatic. Yet dependence is scorned, even in intimate relationships, as though dependence were incompatible with self-reliance rather than the only thing that makes it possible."*

—Adam Philips & Barbara Taylor,
quoted in Maggie Nelson's *The Argonauts*

RIGHT RELATIONSHIP IS THE ASSOCIATION OF AUTONOMOUS individuals who freely choose to be with each other and practice intimacy even in the pain that is inherited and felt around sexual relationship. We commit to the primary practice of bodily intimacy within and without to heal the trauma of previous generations and our own. We cannot underestimate the social context of violence and the destruction that has been wreaked on us by people who feel separate from their life. We all carry the trauma of history in us, causing us to avoid relationship—whether we are technically with someone or not. It is the purpose of life to love as the whole body, so it is essential that we actually do that! Without ignoring the clear need for social and economic transformation (for survival, even), we must make a place for ourselves on this Earth and participate in the given wonder of nature. It is a challenge to drop the barriers put up by the social mind and create a relationship of complete intimacy with another. Yet we can do it, because it is natural.

So, I suggest that to enter into appropriate partnership is our first responsibility in life. After about seven years of life and relationship study, experience, and experimentation—ideally at ages 21 to 28, but in practice whenever we come to it—we recommend people choose a monogamous partner, perhaps with the guidance of their teachers. Not casualness or polyamory, the new forms of patriarchy that avoid the fire of polarity and avoid the necessity of giving yourself to the conditions of actual relationship. Not controlling others through the ideal of cool, detached nonchalance. In monogamy, we can go deeply into all that polarity offers to both in the unfolding of our hearts.

When you do feel inclined to practice mutuality with a lover, do everything that you need to do to cut through society's dysfunction. A friend once asked me how a person should tell who to have Sex with. In our convoluted dissociation from our natural instincts, it may not be immediately obvious to us. The answer is that the three Ls must be present in both directions: like, love, and lust. The latter gets a bad rap due to our negative experiences of sexuality devoid of receptivity. Yet genuine desire—polarity and its chemistries—*is* the nurturing force of life, and the entire natural world including us is participating in it constantly. Life is only interested in the continuity of life. Mother Nature came up with an excellent means to ensure that all species flourish and evolve: the absolute attraction of opposites. Reality moves through us as these forms for this purpose. Life *is* Sex. The pollen in the air is the Sex of plants. The flowers and the sounds of animals are the Sex of nature. No matter how convoluted the human mind becomes, we are still this condition. We do not need to 'become' anything in order to have a free and healthy life. There is nothing to be liberated from.

The initial hormones of desire are nature's way of ensuring we get together. After approximately three months, however, they wear off and we are faced with the need to transform our intimacy into adult loving if we want to continue in the polarity. Otherwise, the weight of social patterning threatens to take over. How do we do this? Make time for intimacy, including actual sexual loving. Enjoy the things that brought you together in the first place. Do things with each other that are pleasurable—hobbies, music, boating, community events, travel, the arts, friends, walks—and make love. Sexual loving is a discipline of pleasure but a discipline no less, because we tend not to do it. Culture has prioritized everything else over intimate sexual union, so we tend to let social priorities, work expectations, and children take over. Action is required. We must do our loving. The mind must take a back seat to the intelligence of the body and let the life current flow between intimates. Commit to practicing intimacy in deeply held personal, private, and sacred circumstance. Reach out and touch your intimate partner. No matter what is going down, make a tangible physical link. The energy moves. After that, you are away. It is bodily loving that heals the wounds of unlove. Someone has to lead the way. Give in to your partner and just do it, like the exhale is given to the inhale.

To participate in the inherent union of God and Sex, there needs to be a relationship of continuity, where there is no question of whether each is there for the other. This is called commitment. But real commitment arises naturally from the depth of pleasure that is intimacy. It is not an enforced ideal or demand but only participation in what is already given. It is not 'needy' or co-dependent to want commitment in your life. Your body is committed to and dependent on air, on light, on water, and on food, and Sex is another of these natural dependencies. The movement towards sexual polarity is not *only* a social one; it is also the most powerful force of nature, and engaging this force reconnects us with what is natural and real. 'Spiritual' people tend to react against the social pressure to be in relationship, without discovering that it is also an entirely natural and unproblematic movement of life to life. We can participate in natural love-dependency without it being anything to do with the social phenomenon of co-dependency, where two people both convinced that God is absent attempt to convince the other to rescue them. Humanity must be given the means of that participation now.

We evolved monogamy in its predominant cultural form, but it retains the trappings of patriarchal ownership models. And so there is another step in that evolution to a place where two people can say "you are my power" to each other, one empowering the other in an endless mutual exchange. One blessing the other in the power of the cosmos that is arising as both. We need this container in order to be steady in the lapping of God's nectar. It cannot be enforced as an ideal but enjoyed only as a gift where the three Ls are present.

A crucial part of intimacy is being together in relaxed enjoyment. It is also vital to spend time alone where we can feel the integrity and completeness of our life as an individual. Too much constant company can diminish the energy between the polar opposites and leave us swimming in casual overfamiliarity. Some time apart, including time with other friends, personal projects, work, days away and particularly one's personal practice, is vital in maintaining the integrity of an independent life.

***

To step outside of the chaos around Sex, we cannot keep engaging with the dysfunction we may have experienced. More attention to the problem will not resolve the problem. Behavioral patterns fall away naturally when they are no longer felt to be necessary. Each person must claim their own life and practice their loving to build something positive amongst the ruins. The process of healing is in relationship with actual other people, particularly in the mutual intimacy between two people who freely choose each other. The more we practice actual intimacy, the more we discover our latent talents for relating to one another. The practice of relationship, including Sex, is the process of all psychological adjustment, self-discovery, and understanding. It is through partnership, the most valuable thing on Mother Earth, that we progressively heal the vulgarity and pain of past sexual behaviors and attitudes. When we place value and dignity on sexual union—the most potent connection we can have with another person—we connect directly to the source of life. We recognize each other as the power of the cosmos and participate in that fact.

Be prepared, however: in the course of our daily relational lives there are clearly difficulties and pain. Because receptivity has been socialized out of men, most have learned to behave in aberrant ways to try and 'get' what they have been trained out of feeling. In response, women have learned to be defensive only. Love brings up everything that is unlove to be seen and understood. In other words, as we embrace our relationships, much buried emotion may surface. It is like opening dusty old filing cabinets. This is why intimacy is so difficult, rewarding, and fiery! The process can be disturbing as all of society's dysfunction and the pain in one's family lineage rears its head in order to be released. Deep pain is felt around Sex due to the lack of receptivity we have all experienced, and intimacy will uncover these feelings. Intimate sexual relationship demands that we have the capacity to see, receive, understand, and let go of each other's inherited trauma. Trauma is a popular modern word for what some cultures have called karma, and we release it for ourselves, for our ancestors, and for future generations simultaneously. Coming into relationship is a challenge that is within our grasp. We are in a great nurturing force, and we can move into our natural state and relinquish the patterns of the past that have been imposed on us. Acknowledgement of the pain is a healing process.

It is our practice of intimacy with ourselves, within which we process and meet our emotional experiences, that prepares us to be intimate with another. Intimacy with body, breath, and relationship in that order. Healing society's patterns can be a slow turning, but I promise you, an appropriate bodily practice of intimacy (the union of inhale and exhale) speeds it up incredibly. Co-ordinated moving and breathing practice returns us to actual and natural participation in what is real and disintegrates the patriarchal impositions that make stable relationship impossible. The visceral changes for both men and women quickly arise as the nervous system becomes receptive through the frontal line. Even penetration becomes a completely receptive and sensitive function in the total context of receptivity.

It is shocking how so many great spiritual teachers never even mention Sex and relationship, let alone acknowledge it as the basic method of transformation (and the way in which they entered the world). On the other side of the problem, the exaggerations of so-called tantric or 'sacred' Sex teachers are just creating more false desires and public confusion. Whether it is new or old-world religion, mindfulness meditation, popularized yoga, dance, shamanic medicine ceremonies, or the myriad offerings of our secular world, there is scarce training for successful and honest sexual intimacy. Nor is there acknowledgement that intimacy with all ordinary conditions is the means to know reality or God. I offer this way forward with inconsolable sadness and overwhelming empathy for all of us who still suffer the pain of the denial of life and the male dominance that does not completely receive the feminine—the body, the emotions, the fullness of mind, nature, and real desire unhooked from social limitations.

***

If you find yourself in partnership without mutuality, be unconcerned. We acknowledge that inherited obstructive patterns and pain can run deep. Sometimes they can get intertwined and too complex between couples. The complexity may prevent the love from doing its work. The way to decide whether to stay together with someone is when you both definitely want to, but sometimes we must acknowledge that amidst each other's different patterns and circumstances, all the loving that can be done, has been done. We have inherited a lot of pain that sometimes the loving from two conscientious people will not shift. Don't be too hard on yourself or your partner. In learning a new skill, like a musical instrument, it is necessary to make mistakes before we learn how to make harmony. It is necessary to know when to move on and do your loving with another, and then you can be free of the torture of ambiguity. After a long time of testing, it can be most appropriate to separate, with the same sacred gratitude in which you came together. (In fact, serial monogamy is our present social norm in the West, and it is best to acknowledge this and end the blame game that occurs in most separations or the sense of personal failure that may grip you.) You will not leave casually, but do not look back to do your loving in the sentimental past. Do it here and now with someone who may meet you in body, mind, and heart. Be prepared to have it all with them. Do not hold back based on past failures and fears, most of which are not your own.

When we have a long history in a partnership, there comes a point in life where you may not want to leave the other even where there is no polarity in the body-mind. If that is the case, stay together and love them for the life that they are. Love for love's sake. True love is to be untroubled by the limitations of the one we love. There is no point in life where you cannot truly receive another, no matter who they are.

We have to admit that the dysfunctions of our society have gone deep, and appropriate relationship may not be forthcoming. If you find yourself single and yearning for relationship, keep practising on your own and then put yourself out there. Recruit every kind of help from family, friends, and professionals to find yourself a mutual partner. Be clear on what you are looking for and do not sit under anyone's table waiting for scraps. Intimate relationship is the natural development and fulfilment of your own practice of intimacy with yourself. The force of mutuality must have its way! Meet all kinds of people and bring every relationship to a kindly friendship of mutual trust before moving into Sex. Explain to every potential partner your view and intention on all of this; use the discussion within these pages to begin an honest and real dialogue. Should intimate relationship with another person not arise, celebrate! You are saved the dreadful inconvenience of having to try to purify civilization's patterns and obstructions to intimacy that inevitably arise in all relationships. Then it is just you and the universe, and this intimacy with everything is what you can celebrate. Ignore the endless social pressure that suggests you are less if not in relationship. It's just you and God (and that indeed is a catalyst that may well bring somebody to you to do your loving with). Either way, it's all good.

## Radiating from the Core of Your Loving

My observation is that in regular social life there is really only one thing going on. People want to get paired up and have access to Sex and the comfort of Sex and friendship. Once that is in place, all other relationships are reduced to little or no importance. It's probably biological, an arrangement based on the need to actually procreate in suitable circumstance, and nothing wrong with that! And it is the need for companionship in a socially limited and dysfunctional world. People get into relationship as security and defense against the world. This is what is going on and it is hard to deny it or say it is wrong. These social behaviors are certainly a limit on energy and potential, however. When that's what you're doing, it dampens down the capacity to love, as you're doing relationship as a defensive protection mechanism, rather than as a rich container for intimacy. A fulfilled life requires that we understand this limit on life and intimacy and go beyond isolating pair-dependency, so our love is not confined to a certain direction but can extend to everyOne and everything everywhere in the One absolute condition of reality in which all others and every 'thing' is happening. This does not mean that we should abandon exclusive Sex relationship, because any form other than monogamy is generally socially dysfunctional, but with our partner we can understand what the problem of the tendency toward pair-isolation is and allow each other to be turned outward into relationship with all and everybody else. How wonderful to have each other *and* have everyOne else as well.

You allow each other autonomy and develop personal interests and close friendships with a range of people, each in your chosen directions. Partnership is a matter of choosing each other freely and enjoying wonderful time together, shared interests, and bodily intimacy. It is not a substitute for the total connection to reality (that which beats the heart and moves the breath and Sex) or an attempt to find it with each other exclusive of all other connections. It is an opportunity to feel and express that reality-connection together and to extend the enjoyment felt in your relationship to all other relationships. Enjoy your relationship with a frequency you both agree upon while extending your love-regard to the whole world. The energy that you cultivate in your intimate partnership with each other soon begins to radiate in all directions. The power of your loving is 'love fuel' for your work in the world and enables you to love and serve others endlessly.

The autonomy of your daily practice of intimacy with body and breath goes a long way towards ensuring that you feel intimacy with life itself in and as all relationship. No longer trying to grasp it in your partner in limiting social co-dependence.

# CHAPTER TWENTY-THREE

## *Regenerative Intimacy*

*Embraces are Comminglings: from the Head even to the Feet:*
*And not a pompous High Priest entering by a Secret Place.*
—William Blake, Jerusalem

SEX* IS THE HEART'S ACTIVITY, AND THE GREATEST APHRODISIAC is intimacy. There may be some stimulating emotional feelings in the sense of being desired by another, especially if we feel lonely or unworthy, but this is not what I mean by intimacy. Intimacy is the flow of mutuality and delight as we participate in the natural chemistries and energies of life. It is the whole-body experience of love. Intimacy is not a casual affair. The very word implies a connection beneath the surface of things; its original meaning was 'most inward or deep seated.' It is an opportunity to participate in the life of another. By doing so, you participate positively with the powerful, regenerative function of nature. Respect for yourself, your body, and the preciousness of Sex

* Some may wonder why we use the somewhat confronting word 'Sex', rather than sticking to the favored euphemisms 'making love' or 'sleeping together.' It is because our embarrassment and avoidance of the word Sex is a direct proof of how it has been toxified. The word itself can hardly be used without it implying something negative or sleazy. I feel these euphemisms often try to bypass the dysfunction and vulgarity that Sex has become in an attempt to delude ourselves that everything is okay.

supports a social order based on love and nurturing instead of control and denial. Those who have been in a committed partnership come to realize that Sex with sincere affection is the most extraordinary human experience. It is something that simply cannot be achieved by manipulating Sex as philosophy or as a method of seeking. No, Sex is the most basic connection of life, the union of opposites in our own form that reveals the source of opposites. Without intimacy, the physical act of Sex does not measure up. It is unfulfilling and even painful. It is no wonder people are giving it up.

Now more than ever, we must deal with our Sex. It is where we are stuck; it is the knot we must all undo one way or another. We still carry the weight of history's spiritual and religious attempts to bypass Sex, whether we are religious or not. Hidden medieval thought structures prevail in us that assume Sex, the body, and life itself are sinful, and that God is apart, above, or within in a higher realm of purity. This is mad, because we are already the purity of life occurring. No one can be more purely Life than anyone else. It's just not possible. Whether we deny Sex through casual promiscuity, fearful guilt and shame, or an attempt at spiritually sanctioned celibacy, we must turn this around and become completely Sex positive.

The first point to consider when addressing our Sex is that because of our dysfunctional social inheritance, each person in a sexual relationship needs to have a simple practice that heals and restores the system to the natural state. On a daily basis, we participate in the relatedness of the whole body with everything in existence. The mind is felt to be connected to the heart; the base of the body is felt to be connected to the trunk; no aspect of our body/mind has any existence independent of the whole. The body is strong yet soft and responsive. The inhale is linked to the quality of receptivity: the breath sensitizes the feeling front of the body so that it has the capacity to receive our experience, our life, and ultimately another person in sexual union. The exhale is linked to the quality of strength: we feel the support of the legs, base, and spine as the breath moves from the base of the body. We just naturally, non-obsessively participate in the essential mutuality of life—strength and receptivity, stability and sweetness. Then we can simultaneously receive and give to our partner in the intensity of relationship and sexual embrace. We bring our loving to our partner. They receive it and surround us with love. We then have more love to give to our partner. That is the empowering process and it is endless. It is why it is said in the traditions that two people can bring each other to God. A literal flow of feeling through the whole body like a great river, nurturing and cleansing, broad and dependable, a vehicle for all of life's activities around it. In the instinctual harmony of intimacy we know God, the heart blooming as all. But in the pain that is felt around sexual relationships, this is a hard pill to swallow. Without a practice of intimacy with our own body and breath, it's likely that our system will not be prepared or 'tuned' to hold sufficient energy. Life energy *is* sexual energy; they are one and the same.

## Down and Out

Sex has been degraded with a dreadful ordering around male 'pleasure,' a stress-release emptying of the base in the ending of his own desire—with no life connection, no sensitivity, and no receptivity of feminine radiance, which is the very power of life and God. Conventional sex valorizes orgasm and the ending of desire as the organizing principle. When there is an urgency toward orgasm, particularly prevalent in men, and Sex routinely ends with one or both partners spilling their energy down and out from the base of the body, then over time both partners are likely to lose interest in Sex, as it is felt to be a depleting, tiring activity. Some people even find themselves unconsciously resenting their partner for 'stealing' their energy and withdraw emotionally. In such emptying there is neither ascent nor descent of the life current, just a draining of energy from a system that is not receiving. Many people fall asleep straight away in their feeling of depletion. Top athletes are instructed not to ejaculate before important events because of this depleting effect. We all want more energy, but when the sexual energy flows through us, it just hits our blockages like a river against boulders and causes agitation. Our body cannot hold the energy and there is a tense rush toward orgasm (for both men and women).

So we must learn to receive. We release our obstacles in the surge of life that flows through us at all times. We can then abide within the sexual flow without drama or aggressive haste. Our direct participation in the union of inhale and exhale enables us to receive, and the resulting intimacy with all ordinary aspects of Mother Nature releases our blockages. We become capable of receiving our experience, rather than reacting to it. The release of obstacles is refined and completed in intimate sexual life with someone of your choice.

We discover that the pleasure is in the flow of feeling between lovers, not in the ending of desire. Try occasionally bypassing orgasm and see what happens. Walk away while you are still full of energy and enjoy the feeling of fullness in your system. This is the natural flow of life and we can learn to participate in it constantly. Men and women can experiment with relaxing the base of their body during loving, with a light tensing of the muscles of the perineum to help move energy up the spine and avoid depleting, down-and-out orgasm. Exhalation may help relax tension. But please don't take these ideas as techniques and get all weird about it. The impulse to circulate the life current occurs naturally in the prior feeling of whole-body intimate connection. The principle 'method' is to completely love your intimate partner as the very power and unfathomable beauty of life.

The idea of retaining ejaculation is not useful outside of the context of honest descent and ascent and real love of your partner. In reaction to conventional orgasm, some modern spiritual subcultures have made philosophy out of retaining ejaculation, demonizing the ejaculatory function as a loss of energy to be forcefully avoided at all costs. This is practiced within the belief system of attempting to ascend and transcend, to conquer the base of the body and 'sublimate' energy up the spine. I want to tell you that only in descent, the receiving of your lover, is there stable male ascent that is authentic. The gathering of descending energy in the whole body creates the effortless surge of ascent. And I mean the literal ascent, the literal arising of lingam, as well as energetic. Ascent does not require sublimation or denial of the body base, sometimes thought of as the lower chakras. When the ascension (including literal male penetration) occurs in the total context of receptivity, it is no longer an assertive, insensitive, or intrusive action; it becomes a literal part of receptivity. There is no final healing of yoni without the synchronistic healing of lingam to receive. Then Sex becomes loving, honest and real, the ardent collaboration between two people, neither of whom is subordinate to the other. Both strong and giving. Both utterly receptive. Not threatened or on guard, but completely participatory in the surge of giving and receiving that is life itself. It is true for both men and women, in same-sex or opposite-sex intimacy. In this regenerative flow, ejaculation can be economized in natural cycles, or with practice even experienced without a loss of energy as a movement in and up rather than down and out. Especially if it is synchronistic with your intimate's orgasm, the energy will move through to the crown rather than be thrown out. If a sportsperson were to learn to receive (the descent), their Sex would become ascending energy that would be completely regenerative and energizing and invigorate their sports occasion. Likewise, all activity of our lives is energized through true sexual intimacy. Sex becomes a source of energy, rather than a depleting activity or a lustless 'duty' to your partner.

Ejaculation must occur in a natural frequency for the body's health, less frequently as we get older. Bypassing ejaculation is not particularly relevant to a young man, although it is good to experiment with it. In the early time of youthful relationships, just have good loving sex. You have lots of energy for it. As you get older, say in your thirties, experiment more with retaining ejaculation. As the years go by it will become a more pertinent consideration. To make love frequently in later years, bypassing ejaculation becomes an imperative. The frequency of ejaculation diminishes to about once a week in your thirties and to once or twice a month in your forties and fifties and beyond. Yet you may be making love daily. There is simply no need to throw off the energy. We step out of the usual lifestyle patterns of depletion.

A form of progress has been to insist on women's right to also participate in down-and-out stress-release orgasm, rather than function only in service to the male's. Both partners experiencing this is seen as the ultimate achievement. At least this is an improvement on woman being the mere context for male fulfilment. But Sex is not a form of polite turn-taking where each person gives until their partner reaches orgasm and then takes their turn to reach orgasm themselves. The pleasure is in the simultaneous movement of feeling, the circulation of energy between lovers. This is what we value and enjoy. Sex is a constant state of giving and receiving. Increased receptivity obviously increases the strength in the systems and the sharing of that strength. There is a waxing and waning of the male/female energies and at times movement will deepen according to the changing flow of feeling. Each partner practices receiving and giving simultaneously to an absolute degree of feeling. Each moment is so pleasurable that we relax into the moment, into the pleasure, and it is full and sufficient. We transcend the need to urgently orgasm or the need to stressfully repress our orgasm. We simply relax. Should you become so full and relaxed that your feeling resolves in the blossoming of an orgasm, so be it. Then it will not be depleting; rather, it will be an energetic thrill to the whole body and will move through both intimates as waves of feeling. Once a woman has learned how to relax into the feeling of being safely and sensitively received without the urgent drive towards tension release, she can have as many deep orgasms as occur naturally. Her partner will enjoy all of them. They are as much his as hers. They are mutually shared and the participation of one partner increases the energy in the other. He learns to be responsive to her movement. He receives her energy and movement as a woman does man. Yet he remains strong and present to her as she receives him. There is a gathering of the energies by the nurturing female aspect of each person. And each receives the fullness of the male strength in the other.

The pleasure of man is not in his own pleasure, but in the pleasure of his partner. This can be understood in many ways. In heterosexual union it is specifically true that the deeper the pleasure of the woman, the deeper the man enjoys her and the loving. So, the man's secret is to please his woman and learn the sensitivities required to get viscerally connected and please her. The deeper her release, the deeper will be his. He is there for her as strength, yet at the same time he is a soft and receptive vehicle for her own movement. In day-to-day life he is there for her in the same way. The true meaning of the word husband is to till or cultivate, to gather in the energies of your partner.

All of the above applies to same-sex intimacy, as the male and female energies within each person interact in the movement of strength and receptivity. Each partner's strength is received and gathered by the other and returned in the flow of feeling; each partner learns to relax into the movement of the sexual current and not rush hurriedly toward orgasm; and each partner tunes in to the pleasure of the other and tangibly enjoys this for themselves. Same-sex intimacy is not immune to patriarchal dynamics—no matter the sex or gender of lovers, when the function of strength is exaggerated at the expense of the function of receptivity, Sex becomes abusive of the feminine (within all). All people regardless of sex or gender are capable of insensitive and aggressive penetrating energy. Empowerment of woman may be mistaken to mean expressing sexual aggression equal to what they have received from the male. Therefore, the need to make all strength unequivocally receptive is relevant to all forms of intimacy.

In regular culture, men are encouraged to aggressively penetrate women, who are encouraged to be a passive receptacle for the man's need to release built-up tension. As a result, there is a special responsibility during lovemaking for men to withhold their forceful movement so that a woman's forceful movement and strength may develop. He does this by slightly or almost completely withdrawing while maintaining a strong presence for her with a slower movement. The penetration remains in energetic form. The movement may quicken but with less penetration to allow her male force to come through and allow him to gather her energy. With each partial withdrawal her energy will be thrown into his body and up his back and spine to the crown, while he receives and embraces her female aspect in the soft front of the body. The spine is the vehicle for the male force, while the front is the receptive female aspect—in every body. It turns out that the base of the body is as holy as the crown of the body, and that the realization of God depends on the whole body, in all its aspects and functions. The whole body is the heart, unfolding in all directions.

## Whole-Body Loving

As we embrace with the whole body, there is not an exclusive focus on the genitals, nor an embarrassed avoidance. Indeed, the whole body is an erogenous zone, and most people respond powerfully to being touched or caressed in places other than just the genital region. Just as we find through the movement of the breath through the body, no part of the body exists independently. During Sex every part of the body is in co-operation. The soft area of the chest and breasts receives our lover, while the head, as an extension of the heart, may speak with heartfelt expressions. The breasts, too, both male and female, conduct the flow of nurturing from the heart through the upper body and crown above, between the two bodies and beyond. The soft, feeling area of the face and lips can receive and express, and the eyes can receive and give. The eyes should not fixate or stare. Gaze is relaxed and free to move. The eyes can open and close spontaneously in the feeling of the embrace; the visual experience is not the main source of Eros, nor is it denied in embarrassment. The heart and the head are the primary area of focus within the embrace. The great base of the body moves in co-operation with the heart. We move according to our needs and desires. The spine is awake. As the pleasure intensifies and deepens, we can adjust to each other spontaneously—except the 'other' is no longer an other. If necessary, we can be very still while the life current moves through us, or even not touch at all but just enjoy the nurturing flow from the heart through the whole body through each other. The love-making will end intuitively and not through the ending of desire. We rest side by or side, sleep, or move on and continue to revel in the intensity of the life current as it moves through and pleasures the system. There will not be a tortured feeling of wanting to end desire and depolarize the system. We abide within the ongoing charge of the polarity. It's all about opening bodies and nervous systems to receive each other's strengths, gifts, and subtle energies. It's about your whole body being able to feel *all* that can be felt, opening yourself to life and love through breath and movement. It is the possibility of whole-body absorption one to another in the nurturing flow of life. This is the meaning of 'love thy neighbor as thyself' in its most vital essence, revealing the great gift that life offers.

The entire act of sexual mutuality is organized around strength and receptivity, the natural polarities that our systems and all of nature are expressing. All female and male qualities exist simultaneously, equally, and dependently. When we love as the whole body, socially imposed limitations on gender function and qualities are corrected by the male/female union developed within our systems. Our culture has privileged strength to the detriment of receptivity. As a result, it is useful perhaps to have some pointers on how to heal this imbalance. But this is not about method or technique. It is about love. It is what two bodies do that love each other. The bodies know what to do. Love is a real biochemical process. So do not worry about this and do not attempt to apply it as a directive or method. Everything happens naturally in time. In this regard, the most precious 'technique' a person has to transcend depleting orgasm is their love of their partner.

In fact, in our culture there is extreme obsession with technique. Various devices, toys, and add-ons are sold as tools to improve upon the act of bodily loving. These accessories are likely to be sought after because a relationship lacks intimacy or partners do not feel received by one another. When one or both partners experiences numbness or dissociation in their body, depleting orgasm, and loss of interest in Sex over time, the drive to 'spice things up' arises. In the fullness of sexual mutuality between lovers there is really no need for a large inventory of stimulating add-ons or exaggerated positions. The relationship itself is full and complete and contains everything that is needed for regenerative intimacy, the shared participation in the broad and deep flow of sexual feeling between intimates. And as the relationship develops, the pleasure and depth of the bodily loving also deepens. When the whole body is fully functioning in life as life in its union with the opposite, within and without, the heart is felt. It is the heart on the right, the culminating point of body and mind, where above and below have merged absolutely in a measureless depth of feeling. God and Sex are realized as one. Some consider this to be a 'spiritual' heart, somehow transcending the body. But it is only felt in the body, as the body, as life in its tangible and unobstructed relationship with everything including especially the union from which life comes.

There is no requirement to orgasm. Orgasm has been prized in conventional Sex as some kind of goal or purpose. Many women are burdened with a sense of lack through finding it difficult or impossible to achieve down-and-out orgasm. Remove that as a goal, *completely.* Relax into the feeling of pleasure that *is* there, whatever it is. Any tension you may feel has been a valid response to the world's dysfunction. You may just be too refined for the usual stress-release approach. Both partners release the sense of there being a goal and relax into the pleasure of intimate affection. Over time, in that relaxing and participation in the pleasure, there can be a resolve in the nurturing force of life that shudders through the whole body like waves and becomes quiet. Perhaps very subtly. This is not something to be attained, but something that may be enjoyed in the continuity of your loving. There is no goal to loving. So release any sense of identity you may have as someone who does or does not orgasm, or who does or does not 'give' orgasms to a partner. It is all turning Sex into a stressful activity towards a future result, eclipsing the pleasure that is already there.

It is also not necessary to spend a long and exhausting time on Sex. In the early stages of life and relationship this will probably be natural, but as the physical loving does its work in the system, the necessity for long sexual intimacy will probably diminish. This is not necessarily a sign of reduced intimacy, but may rather be a sign of our merging with our partner. We may find the vibratory energy of partners seems to be in each other, refined and stable. "You are in my spine." In this case little physical loving is necessary, although some touch is probably always enjoyable. Work out all such agreements with sensitivity to the needs of each person in this mutual understanding. Loving has an accumulative effect on the loving you do. The body blooms open and relaxes more and more. Also, know that the practice of Sex will change as life goes on. There is a change from robust movement in earlier life to a more subtle movement of energy as life unfolds. The requirement for physical embrace may diminish. All that work has been done. Now, you rest and abide in the feeling and the flow of the relationship. It is the relationship itself which is the pleasure, the gift of life. When the pleasure pathways have been opened through loving, the energy or spirit pathways are opened, as they are one and the same. God and

Sex are one. We know God through embracing Sex and all ordinary conditions of relatedness. There really may be less need for lovemaking. The life current is already established and you are enjoying its flow. Words, touch, dance, or sleeping together may be as powerful (yet the energy will be finer, like a silk thread) as Sex was earlier.

## Riding the Wave

Our bodies are nature, and nature is a sublime intelligence, beyond anything we can artificially approximate. The sexual current flowing through us, as us, is the intelligence of nature, and she has her own nurturing agenda for our lives and healing, including for our sexual intimacy. Because we are all male-female, the male programing to 'get,' control, and own the feminine is an issue within each one of us, in the form of the dissociative mind trying to dominate the intelligence of the body. In practice, this looks like trying to control the life current, rather than move with it (whether in our own body or in relation to someone else's). This is the norm: we absorb so many ideas of what Sex should look like, what our bodies should look like, and what we think another person expects of us, that Sex turns into a performance, rather than just a process of receiving and bathing in the flowing current. Anytime you are performing something, rather than feeling it authentically, you are building dams and irrigation projects that obstruct your own wild flow. We need to stop trying to harness the feminine, control the feminine, channel, sublimate, dominate, or subjugate the feminine. Just receive and abide in the feminine, and she will take you places. You ride the pleasure of intimacy like riding a wave. You can't be too demanding. Just adapt yourself to the changing flow of the wave. Just so, in order to make our Sex honest we must be willing to abide in not knowing what is going to happen. The great poet John Keats called it 'negative capability': the ability of a writer to be in uncertainty, not imposing a mental agenda on the open ground of creative intuition. In the context of Sex, it means we do not need to strategically move or perform anything at all. In the healing flow of intimacy, and from our relaxed stillness, trust that authentic movement will arise. It may be joyful embrace, or it may be sincere release of tears. It may be eccentric, wild, or infinitely still. We need a safe container of relationship in order to move with the unpredictable and vulnerable directions of our autonomous feeling. We develop trust in life and in our partner's ability to receive us. The surfer rides delicately but surely: strength receiving.

## CHAPTER TWENTY-FOUR

# *Overcoming Obstructions*

*O Shame O strong & mighty Shame I break thy brazen fetters*

—William Blake, *Jerusalem*

We have a few major concerns that commonly obstruct free and totally Sex-positive intimacy. These are: fear of unwanted pregnancy, fear of sexual disease, fear of sexual aggression and experiences of sexual abuse, and fear of abandonment. Sexual education in schools cultivates the first two fears, rather than giving practical information in a Sex-positive environment. How could it be otherwise, when the teachers themselves don't have it sorted.

### Fear of Unwanted Pregnancy

It is the responsibility of both partners to protect against unwanted pregnancy. Men have been used to getting Sex and letting women carry the burden of responsibility on their body and their mind. Women of our world generally have not been able to trust men to take responsibility for this, and so they live and love in fear. Even when with a responsible man, it may still be hard for them to trust, due to previous experience. In the centuries of association of women with reproduction and the body (Sex), and men with 'higher' matters (God), we have been conned into thinking conception is wholly a female concern, as if the male is only incidentally involved. Women are suffering the burden of contraceptive responsibility *and* unwanted pregnancies *and* neurotic social scrutiny of their sexual and reproductive choices. A woman can only fully and finally relax into her sexual peace and bliss when it is known that contraception is taken care of. When the man takes responsibility for this, to an absolute degree, his woman can relax. As couples develop their regenerative sexual intimacy, the whole body becomes integrated, with the genitals no longer having an urgent life of their own. Here a man becomes comfortable loving as the whole body without the urgent need for ejaculation. This is the best way to prevent unwanted pregnancies without imposing anything on a woman's body or hormonal system. Until there is complete certainty and competence in the practice of bypassing ejaculation, use condoms. The complaint over minimal loss of sensation through condom use only arises where there is no whole-body feeling and participation. Sex is not merely the stimulation of the genitals. We sincerely urge every body to avoid pharmaceutical or mechanical interventions on the female body, which are another form of patriarchal dominance on the feminine from men who do not want to take responsibility for their reproductive function. Having not taken responsibility for his reproductive function, man is in no position to have opinions or make laws concerning women's reproductive choices. The obsessive interest on such matters would be better focused on sorting out relationships and giving all people the education and tools to receive one another with love and maturity.

### Fear of Disease

Sexually transmitted diseases and illnesses are a reality we cannot ignore. Please do not let fear of disease obstruct you from enjoying the fullness of your sexual loving. Until you know that your partner is not carrying a sexual illness, feel free to use condoms for your loving. Use your medical clinicians to diagnose and treat all possibilities before not using a condom, but do not hesitate to do your loving. The ardent loving and sharing of energy between two lovers helps bring health to the entire biochemistry of your life, including the immune function. And this healing power of life helps to outshine illness and potential illness. Sexual disease should be discussed freely between partners, and divorced from any sense of shame if possible. Do not let the fact it is 'sexual' make you all ghoulish and screwed up with embarrassment. There is no point compounding the issue with shame. Think of it the way you would a physical issue with any other part of the body. The threat of disease has long been used to frighten people away from Sex, often with religious motivations. False connections are made implying that disease is punishment from God for sexual activity, a cruel argument. It is not so long ago that religious fundamentalists tried to convince the world that AIDS was caused by 'sinful' Sex, rather than by a tragic failure of the immune system. In open and honest discussion, the right precautions can be taken. The container of besotted monogamy and each partner's trust and commitment in this container will help relieve the mind of anxiety about contracting sexual disease. We can relax knowing our partner is committed to us, not out of social obligation or insecure demand, but because the intimacy itself is so valuable and rich. Within the modern culture of casual sex and spiritual ideals of 'giving other people freedom' it can be seen as needy or unspiritual to want to know about your partner's sexual activity. This creates a hotbed for the transmission of sexual disease. In love relationship we share all secrets, not because we have to, but because we want to. It should go without saying that if you are unfortunate enough to contract any such illness, this should never be concealed from your partner.

## Fear of Aggression

If we have experienced sexual aggression, there is likely to be deep fear lodged in our bodies based on this prior pain. Our pain is in response to both overt abuse and to the way everyday people are sexing within the cult of the normal. Our bodies contract, like a sea anemone closing up. The nervous system tenses to protect us from feeling pain, and without conscious resolution and release, we remain this way. This is everyone to some degree. We can see the burden of unprocessed pain weighing down on older people and curling the body in on itself. It is our job to find stable and receptive partnership within which we can relax (the base of the body in particular), knowing we are completely safe from aggressive intrusion (strength without receptivity). In the relaxation, the pain caused by earlier aggression will probably come up to be felt and resolved in the heart—even if we were not aware it was there. It is important to be with someone with whom we feel free to go through the sequence of emotions, not denying any authentic feeling in the desire to impress or appear to be 'easy' or happy all the time. Make sure that you are making real choices in your gentle explorations of relationship. When relationship develops into emphatic friendship and the three Ls are present in that friendship, explore the receptivity of each other, founded on your practice of receiving life through moving and breathing and relaxing. Come together with great respect and receptivity of each other. It is only loving that releases the pain, not avoidance of it. So do your loving, and the pain will be released.

I would not recommend anyone seek out sexual massage or 'dearmoring' as a way to release the body's valid contraction. While it is true that the muscles in the base of the body become tensely held, preventing full flow of feeling and energy, it is best that this is addressed in sincere personal relatedness, in the sacred and safe container of love relationship. There is no point in one person 'opening' only to be retraumatized by the lack of intimacy in the occasion or by a still-insensitive future partner. The blossoming and unfolding must happen together in real and sincere mutual love. Not anyone doing a technique on anyone else, and certainly not within any dynamic of hierarchy (which is inherent in the model of therapist and patient).

We also want to add our heartbroken sympathy to all those who were sexually abused as children—and this is many, many people. Experts in sexual abuse chart how it is possible for the body to experience some physical arousal, even in the midst of the most hideous assaults. This can create devastating associations between sexual feeling and trauma that must be unraveled and healed in adulthood in competent and caring company. With the help of feeling our connectedness to all, it is possible to move through these deep traumas, and I honor my brave friends who have done so. No matter how traumatized or pained, it remains a fact that we are the power of the cosmos, arising presently as extreme intelligence and absolute beauty. We are so sorry that society failed those who wronged you and turned them into abusers. We are so sorry that you had to suffer the ordeal of growing up in a society with no sexual wisdom. Please know that you *are* allowed to reclaim a purely positive sexuality in the fullness of time.

## Fear of Abandonment

Fear of abandonment is a major obstacle to enjoying the flow of intimacy. Most of us experienced an erratic flow of love from our parents, despite their best efforts. This instils a fear of loss of love and a sense of being unworthy of love in our tender nervous systems. As children and young adults, we took on the assumption that we were less than the power of Life/God. We tend to carry these wounds over into our attempts at adult intimacy. The result is that many adults find themselves fearing emotional withdrawal in their partner and associating it with a sense of being unlovable. When relationship ends, it comes with a heavy tendency to confirm the belief we are deeply flawed, something less than God. Our practice of intimacy with the all in all disconfirms this early programing. When we close down to protect ourselves from potentially touching this wound, then the body hardens and is not open to receiving the nurturing flow that is our condition. Just as avoiding pain results in avoiding all feeling, avoiding potential endings by staying armored prevents potential beginnings.

There is no need to be emotionally sadistic, however. We can be discerning and choose to engage only where friendship, trust, and continuity are established. Sex is not a casual matter—opening ourselves to another sexually, we take on all of their patterning and apparent limits. Our heart is an open wound. We take the risk of vulnerability. Be sure you take on that adventure with another person with discernment. It is a devastating risk to love another, to bare our chests and allow our heart to flow freely. The sense of risk comes from fear of the pain of contraction associated with heartbreak. It literally hurts to contract our hearts, but we have more choice here than we think. When someone whom we love leaves us, we do not have to stop loving them. Even if someone dies or behaves in terrible ways or betrays us, we do not have to stop loving. We may not even like a person or approve of their behaviors, but for the sake of our own nervous system we can keep loving them, from a distance if necessary. The normal thing that happens in relationship is that when we feel rejected, we stop loving. Our childhood pain prevents us from recognizing that when another person cannot love us, it is not our fault. This is the worst abandonment, when we contract our own heart. Love fails not when we feel unloved by others, but when we cannot love others. So keep loving. Then the nurturing force of your own heart keeps flowing. That will keep you safe from a sense of abandonment and from the limits of society. Go back and embrace all the personas you were who were hurt and let them know that you're the survivor and they did a wonderful job in getting you here in the midst of difficult circumstances. Praise and love and celebrate all the personas that you were.

### Tiredness / Exhaustion

There is another very common barrier to intimacy: feeling too tired for Sex. This can be because we are just not that interested in the usual depleting Sex. It may have fallen low on the priority list, as mentioned in the previous chapter. But in our stressed and unequal world, it can also be pure exhaustion. Almost everyone is running on empty. Our feeling of dissociation from Life leaves us depleted and stressed, struggling to become something in the belief we are not yet Something. When we are forced to drive our bodies along like tired horses in the struggles of work and responsibilities, we become numb to the flow of intimate connection. If you find yourself 'too tired' for Sex, just relax and do some gentle moving and breathing. Relax from any guilt about what you 'should' be doing. Prioritize rest and the cultivation of receptivity. In intimacy with the breath, we process our own experience and rediscover the regenerating power that is the ever-available nurturing flow of life. We can then rearrange our lives in ways that prioritize intimacy. When the time is right, tune in to the natural movement in the body toward sexual intimacy and engage the 'discipline of pleasure' with your chosen other. Please know that conventional Sex *is* exhausting, in the usual perceived separation of God and Sex and the attempt to bridge this socially fabricated gap. When Sex is restored as pure and sacred full-body loving, it energizes our system rather than depleting it.

***

We can also mention how Sex/body negativity has created vast shame around the completely normal function of menstruation. This negativity comes disguised as all kinds of religious, spiritual, and cultural logics. If the social mind's body negativity has affected you, I recommend seeking out some of the many excellent resources on cyclical wisdom that restore dignity and relaxed sensitivity to the natural cycles and remove any inherited sense of taboo. For men, receiving this natural function in your partner without any embarrassment is part of the healing of the legacy of shame. We embrace all aspects of nature's intelligence. And for women, your practice of participation in the union of the ascent and the descent, combined with the energy that moves through the body in sincere intimacy, can help to reduce menstrual pain by shifting stagnant energy in the base of the body. The downward flow is the sacred descent of life, equally as valid as the ascending current.

When tuning in to the cycles within, be aware also of the broader Moon cycles as they affect changes in bodily rhythms in both man and woman. Spend time under the Moon and aware of what she is up to, receiving her as you receive one another. The Sun is giving and the Moon and everything else is receiving, including us. Allow one another the natural ebb and flow that you allow the Moon. You may allow loving energy to culminate in an intimate occasion on the Full Moon and perhaps be more rested on the new Moon. But there are no rules, only the process of receiving one another in increasingly refined gratitude of relatedness.

## CHAPTER TWENTY-FIVE

# *Intimacy in the Cycles of Life*

*We all come from one another.*

—Kory McAvoy

BIRTH, LIKE SEX AND DEATH, IS ONE OF THE FEW REALMS OF LIFE that the controlling mind has been unable to colonize completely. There is still some wildness here. Sometimes a person's first adult taste of the power of direct intimacy with their experience is when they are naturally immersed in the process of birth. I have many friends who have reported that in giving birth, the perfect union of the ascending and descending current is felt, as the union of opposites takes literal form as new life. If you are a mother who has experienced this, do not fall into the trap of romanticizing your birth experience or anyone else's as an Edenic moment that must then be replicated through diligent spiritual practice or any method whatsoever. Please do not devalue your present wonder by falling for that thought structure. If, in the primal flow of birth, the mind's impositions fell away and you felt your essential immersed and intuitive intimacy with life, then this is still true now, even if the usual mental structures are back in place. We either are the power of the cosmos, or we are not. It's not something that can come and go. Any search to try and replicate birth experiences through mental effort only adds another level of mind to the perfection of reality. And if you did not have experiences of sublimity through birth, be reassured that no matter what the mind is up to, the fact of birth is still perfectly sublime. The body knew what to do and bought new life into this world. You obviously ARE the Creator, and Sex is God's method on Earth.

In the following phase of family life, the best thing you can give to your children is the model of adult intimacy. Because it is so easy to love the children, usually the adult intimacy of the parents is reduced when children come. It is too easy to love each other via the children and forget to be intimate with each other. In the natural cycle of pregnancy, birth, and restoration from birth, couples should plan on intimate time alone together in a frequency that they both agree upon in their lifestyle. Do not compromise on this, as difficult as it might be. Recruit help if you can and keep the polarity of your adult relationship a valid priority. This is not selfish, as it will be a gift to your children, giving them the rare example of functional intimacy. Naturally, there needs to be a significant time of intimacy without penetration following birth. This doesn't mean no sexual intimacy, as the whole body in its embrace can be erogenous, especially in the fullness and joy of pregnancy and new baby. Then, in the natural course of time, couples should come back together in adult whole-body loving.

Hierarchy has been created through historic emphasis on male activity and spiritual pursuits that implied the family life and motherhood were less. For men and women, if you were still in village having Sex, you were somehow less heroic and wonderful than those who had left the village and went to the monastery. Motherhood has been denied, and is not generally valued or considered a real job. So many mothers feel that if they have left the professional workforce, they are no longer a valid or successful person—despite doing the most important job there is. Mothers suffer. And so do fathers. In addition, if there is a breakdown in the adult intimacy, self-esteem can suffer as we feel like this as our personal failure. I want to point out that this is a social dysfunction, not an individual problem. Everyone is doing their best with the information they have at hand and the shoddy circumstances of society. I so frequently hear women say, "I'm just a mother." It breaks my heart to see how in this world secular success is glamourized and rewarded, and the brilliance of motherhood and fatherhood as the nurturing force of life is minimized.

Whether or not our own parents were together, it is likely that we did not have healthy adult intimacy modelled for us. Therefore it is a big step to introduce it in our generation, and requires a conscious choice to start practicing. But anyone can make that choice at any point in their life, and it is truly easy. You will be healing all generations following you. And many indigenous cultures even believe we are healing the generations of the past in our present success.

We are still suffering the medieval Chain of Being where man is believed to be below God and woman is believed to be below man. The woman is already discriminated against in this primitive belief system, and a woman who becomes a mother then suffers additional discrimination—yet a woman who has not given birth is also discriminated against. The best way to cut through these social impositions is to understand that the nurturing force of life, the principle of motherhood, is every person's condition, man or woman. We are all male-female. No one is second or superior to anyone else in the great nurturing flow that is life on Mother Earth. Our intimacy with life will shrug off these medieval thought structures and emotions of the society we were born into. We can then make autonomous life choices that are not shaped by social expectation, whether we become biological parents or not.

## CHAPTER TWENTY-SIX

# *Sex is the Natural State*

*The rigid man uses laws*
*And if people don't like it, force.*
*If the true Tao is lost*
*then morality takes its place.*
*If that fails, we have 'conscience'.*
*When that fades, we get 'justice'.*
*When that disappears, we have the status quo.*
*Confusion reigns.*
The Tao de Ching, attributed to Lao Tsu (chapter 38)*

THERE IS A RADIANCE IN ANYONE WHOSE LIFE IS ENTIRELY SEX positive, and this radiance is everyone's birthright. Such company has been of great benefit in my life. I have found that there is sublime advantage in sitting closely with friends in this consideration. That said, being around anyone whose male-female polarity is resolved in the heart can bring up all kinds of feelings in a person, including a sense of lack or despair, or a feeling of being attracted, repelled, or

* Translation by Man Hi Kwok et al, Element: Brisbane, 1993.

confused. In the context of good friends this is positive, as these feelings arise to be seen, understood, and released. Relaxing into our own perfection allows us to resolve the habits of sexual politics into the profundity of the heart, which is the perfect union of opposites.

Within the body, male and female have no delineation from one another; there are no sexual politics. Ancient cultures came up with the figure of the *ardhanarisvara,* the deity figure who is half man, half woman, to express the perfect balance of male and female that exists within us all. And in many ancient texts, for example the *Samdhinirmocana Sutra,* it states that the body is already in the awakened state. What do we make of that? We can understand it to mean that as life/reality itself, the body is senior to the mind, with mind arising only as a function of the whole body. Everyone is completely loved and completely nurtured in the natural state. We *are* in the natural state, where everything is Sex, fully functioning and harmonized. Life (us) is extreme attractiveness between opposites, arising in radiance as the multiplicity of individuation, like a tree with thousands of leaves moving in all directions. In the natural state we have natural affection for everybody as an expression of this. We cease to obsess over each other's imagined limitations. Life becomes real. This is everyone's actuality and it can be enjoyed—but not attained, because it is already the case.

Fear of the natural state has been planted in us by centuries of philosophers who felt their own troubled emotional state and projected it out onto humanity. Thomas Hobbes, for example, the influential English seventeenth-century thinker, claimed that life was intrinsically a struggle between warring individuals, and was by its nature "nasty, brutish, and short." Therefore, he argued, to avoid "a state of nature," powerful individuals should rule over everyone else using strict laws and punishments. We can take such theories as the philosopher's personal confession of their own mistrust in themselves and life.

We no longer need to subscribe to the remnants of such thinking. When a person is fully and directly involved in their own experience of life, they are able to intuitively feel their own ethics or modes of right behavior relative to all others. Anyone who practices and teaches direct relationship with the nurturing force of reality is inevitably a non-conformist and will follow life's instinctive and naturally respectful ethics, rather than the laws of secular power structures.

The suggestion that all can have a direct relationship with Life's natural ethics is alarming to those who have not yet come to trust their own goodness and the intrinsic goodness of Life and Sex: those who have not experienced direct intimacy with the purity of reality. Codes of sexual ethics, however benevolently couched, assume that Sex is an uncontrollable and *bad* force, something "nasty, brutish, and short," rather than the nurturing and regenerative force of life, freely chosen. When external codes are proposed from the fear of misbehavior, the person's own intrinsic wisdom and connection to all life is put in doubt. Such codes are a despairing alternative to the great instinctive 'strength receiving' that all can come to feel through the healing practices of intimacy: body, breath, and sexual relationship.

With immense sympathy to all of us who have inherited the burden of patriarchy, I propose we do not give up, but participate in the inherent union, where one empowers the other in endless mutual exchange, just as it is in the natural state. Let us practice our hearts out as participation in the union of opposites within and without. Let us reclaim our life by getting through the valid stages of emotion: fear, anger, pain, and grief. Let us not get stuck at any stage, and come instead to honest grief for the dreadful social circumstance passed on to us. From grief, the powers of compassion spontaneously arise for all, and with them the ability to receive each other and experience the peace and power of the heart's flow in the natural state.

## CHAPTER TWENTY-SEVEN

# *Our Responsibility*

*And I'll tell it and think it and speak it and breathe it,*
*And reflect it from the mountain so all souls can see it.*
*Then I'll stand on the ocean until I start sinkin',*
*But I'll know my song well before I start singin'.*
—Bob Dylan, 'A Hard Rain's Gonna Fall'

*Don't become a guru. Don't become one more monkey.*
—J. Krishnamurti to T.K.V. Desikachar

SUPPRESSION OF THE FEMININE HAS BEEN RELIGIOUSLY SANCTIONED to the point where it is part of all of our thought structures. The suppression of individuals by religious leaders or teachers imagining themselves to be authorities, the suppression of women by men, and the suppression of our own embodied intelligence by the social mind is all the same deal. We must return to the primordial religion of humanity, where we participate directly in Life as equals and opposites, one empowering the other, in same-sex or opposite-sex relationship, in any gender identification or none at all within the male-female spectrum of Mother Nature's biologies. The way forward is to simply remove all power structures, within and without. The body throws out the patriarchal that separated God from Sex. We leave the body alone to allow its intrinsic intelligence to function.

Authority may be an ordinary social form required in the transmission of secular knowledge, but not when it comes to matters of the heart. An algebra teacher, for example, is legitimately more of an authority on algebra. But there is no place for the social pattern of secular authority in the sacred life, and all secular power is only there to serve the sacred, which is the freedom of every person. Life is not for information gathering, it is for living. And everybody is already doing their own life. If there is a teaching function in these matters, then it is the teacher's responsibility to make sure the relationship with the student is equitable and negotiable, as students can find it initially difficult to recognize their teachers as equals and ordinary people. The teacher must therefore attain ordinariness, empowered only on the basis of embrace of life itself, not on the basis of a claim of special knowledge, state, attainment, or any other point of difference. The claim of special attainment is inevitably at the expense of everybody else, who are made to believe they are not yet attained. It is the denial of life. The secrets of the universe are already in you, as you. All that a teacher or friend can provide is a supportive context as someone who knows about life in the form of themselves. This is why a real teacher is 'no more than a friend, and no less than a friend.' The teacher is not a social identity, nor even a personal identity. They are the flow of nurturing, a phenomenon of Mother Nature in local community. If there is such thing as guru then it is this function of nurturing, not an identity. The teacher and student both give themselves to the conditions of *actual,* ordinary human relationship, real intimacy in utter equality. It may be almost impossible for many to understand that teachings can be given free of power structures of any kind. Yet it is so.

The thought structure that assumes a teacher of these matters is a 'knower' or an authority must dissolve. The patriarchy creates and thrives on the thought structure that someone knows and therefore others do not. It is the Chain of Being, the form of our whole civilization, and has seeped into the behaviors of the ordinary life, where the male is presumed to be dominant, for example. And it is false. This thought structure and the behaviors it creates must be seen and dissolved for two people to empower each other as equals and opposites—whether teacher and student, or two people in intimate partnership, or parent and child, or any kind of relationship. Without the dissolution of hierarchy, we cannot receive the power of the feminine. The success of powerful men, be it in spiritual or secular worlds, does not lift all people. It enslaves all people. *Clearly*, everyone is already the power, pure intelligence, and unspeakable beauty of the cosmos in perfect and intrinsic harmony with the rest of the cosmos. This is true whether or not it is acknowledged by the mind. We can get with the program or not, but it is still the program. Reality stays reality no matter what the mind is up to. The hierarchy is the problem itself and there is no transmission in it. It is the social dynamic of disempowerment. As Raoul Vaneigem writes:

> The key is within each of us. No instructions come with it. When you decide to treat yourself as the only point of reference, you will cease to be trapped by name dropping—yours or mine—or by deferring to other people's opinions, or by the particular way they see things.

To make our spirituality and sexuality pure and honest, we must dissolve the power structures that sell us patterned behavior toward future ideals and instead participate in our own life-current. We throw out all patterns put in us by orthodoxy and claim our own life. What is left? The intrinsic unity of all life and the flow to all others in gestures of kindness.

Therefore, this book is not a 'something.' It is not a book of patterns, another system, or a pamphlet for a teaching. It points to all the natural perfect harmonies with air, light, water, the green realm, intrinsic male-female, and any as-yet-unseen causes of the cosmos already established. But these would exist perfectly even without this book. We dissolve the belief in God, this book, or anyone as authority (although 'dissolve' does not imply that at any point it is real). There is nothing being taught here. Your body knows what my body knows. It never crosses my mind that I am any different from you or anyone else. There is no membership, no 'in' or 'out'; no belief system, nothing to assimilate—everyone in the world can embrace God and Sex, should they choose. And if not, they are still both. All are encouraged to make their life into participation with reality, and this is accessible to all. It is the primordial religious practice of humanity, before doctrine was formulated as a way to control the public; it is ancient wisdom re-expressed for modern times, received from all my teachers and now passed on to you. It is my intention that the present writing offers a guide for all to embark on this necessary human adventure.

It is our individual and collective responsibility now, in the truest sense of the word: we have the *ability* to *respond* to the dreadful situation we find ourselves in. I urge everybody to investigate this matter, whatever your own cultural background. Please take this writing's logic and merge it with the authority of your own intellect and experience until it is yours or modified by you. Please translate it into your own language, logic, or cultural framework and communicate it to your own demographic. Our world depends on it, and so does the ecology of Mother Earth. Sustainability begins with intimacy with the wild nature of your own body, breath, and Sex. The first place we begin to honor the feminine is within our own body.

God and Sex, the two most loaded words in the world, are already in union, because Sex is the regenerative power of this universe that creates all things and presently exists as all things, including you. Sex is God's method on Earth. We cannot bypass our responsibility to participate lawfully in our own reality. The weight of religious history still presses on us with the hidden assumption that Sex is lesser, so it is up to us to reclaim it as the pure and holy matter that it is: the heart's activity. It is our responsibility to heal the apparent dysfunction and return to the intrinsic harmony that is the nurturing power of life itself. We don't have to philosophize about it, but we do need to do it. Bob says it all in 'A Hard Rain's Gonna Fall.'

We heal the imagined rift between God and Sex when we behold our body, our spouse, our children, our deity, our guru, our mother, our father, our God, and all of our intrinsic relatedness with the natural world, seen and unseen, as the One reality. There is no hierarchy, and because it does not exist, there is no linear process by which authority is transcended. The mistaken belief in God as 'other' is simply no longer relevant as you participate in your own authority as life. You walk out of the tent of the 'knower' with the courage to stand in your own ground and bloom in your own garden as the great exuberant power of life that you are. Life is exploding through you. God and Sex: now we get both.

# ABOUT THE COLLABORATING AUTHORS

**Andy Raba** is a writer and activist currently living in Wellington, Aotearoa/New Zealand. He holds a Master's degree in English Literature specializing in the visionary science fiction of Philip K. Dick. In his time as a university (college) tutor, Andy has seen first-hand the suffering young people experience as they navigate achievement systems and relationships, and is committed to sharing useful words that enable everyone to enjoy the sublimity of a free life of intimacy, friendship, and adventure. Andy works in a suburban library and also teaches Yoga in the city, helping people to connect with their autonomous life through breath. His writing works to reinvest the mundane with value, as a seamless continuation of his social activism and commitment to giving ordinary people a chance to enjoy their lives.

**Rosalind Atkinson** is from Aotearoa/New Zealand, and works alongside Mark at teaching events around the world. She is a scholar of English Literature, with an MA in mystic poetry from Victoria University of Wellington, and has presented on the subject at conferences around the world and contributed to academic and general publications. After careers including a costume illustrator on the *Hobbit* films, a sailor on youth empowerment tall ships, and an environmental activist, including as crew on the *Rainbow Warrior III* on fisheries and climate change campaigns, Rosalind realized we need to learn how to honor nature in our own forms before we can effectively care for it in 'other' forms. Her activism now comprises sharing tools and words to help each person recover from the global disease of hardheartedness that has dissociated us from our own suffering, other people's suffering, and the planet's suffering. This mission converges with her study of Vedanta and Yoga over the last decade, and she is deeply grateful to Mark and his teachers for their help in freeing these explorations from the socially indoctrinated struggle toward a future result.

You can read more of Andy and Rosalind's writings at www.thedirt.media.

# SOURCES

"A Hard Rain's A-Gonna Fall" by Bob Dylan. Copyright 1963 by Warner Bros. Inc. Copyright renewed 1991 by Special Rider Music. International copyright secured. Reprinted by permission.

Extracts from the poetry of William Blake from *The Complete Poetry and Prose of William Blake.* Ed. David Erdman. Rev. ed. Garden City: Anchor, 1982. Full text available online at http://erdman.blakearchive.org/

*Please note: The utterances of our mystics of popular culture, known and unknown, express the same truth of reality in our own time as did the great mystic poets and sages of previous ages in their time. The utterances that have come down to us from the past are those that could swim through culture's net, so therefore mostly male. There have been many, many women mystics of the ages forgotten as the patriarchy took no regard of them. This has finally changed. There have also been many male mystics speaking for the feminine, embodied intimacy rather than transcendence, who were obliterated by orthodoxy. Further, there is obviously a bias towards those speaking in the English language in this book, due to it being the native language of the authors, but mystic expression has come in all language and all cultures.*

www.ingramcontent.com/pod-product-compliance
Lightning Source LLC
LaVergne TN
LVHW042358150826
845671LV00023B/389/J

* 9 7 8 0 4 7 3 4 8 5 9 1 7 *